SEIZE THE DAY

ROBERT GRIFFITH

Copyright © 2025 Grace and Truth Publishing

All rights reserved. No part of this book may be reproduced, stored in a retrieval system, or transmitted in any form, without the written permission of Grace and Truth Publishing.

GRACE AND TRUTH PUBLISHING
PO Box 338, Gunnedah NSW 2380 Australia
www.graceandtruthpublishing.com.au

All Bible quotes are from the New International Version (NIV) expect where otherwise stated.

NEW INTERNATIONAL VERSION (NIV), Copyright 1973, 1978 and 1984 by international Bible Society. Used by permission of Zondervan Publishing House. All rights reserved.

Other version quotes are from:

AMPLIFIED BIBLE (AMP), Copyright © 1954, 1958, 1962, 1964, 1965, 1987 by The Lockman Foundation. Used by permission.

ENGLISH STANDARD VERSION (ESV), Copyright © 2001 by Crossway Bibles, a division of Good News Publishers. Used by permission. All rights reserved.

NEW AMERICAN STANDARD BIBLE (NASB), Copyright © 1960, 1962, 1963, 1968, 1971, 1972, 1973, 1975, 1977, by The Lockman Foundation. Used by permission.

NEW KING JAMES VERSION (NKJV), Copyright © 1979, 1980, 1982, by Thomas Nelson Inc. Used by permission. All rights reserved.

THE MESSAGE (MSG), by Eugene Peterson, Copyright © 1993, 1994, 1995, 1996, and 2000. Used by permission of NavPress Publishing Group. All rights reserved.

REVISED STANDARD VERSION (RSV), Copyright © 1973, by Thomas Nelson Inc. Used by permission. All rights reserved.

ISBN 978-1-7635504-5-2

TABLE OF CONTENTS

1. Close your eyes and see 4
2. Dealing with the past 16
3. Are you connected? 25
4. A nation in decline 35
5. Have you seen Jesus? 45
6. Bloom where you're planted 54
7. Breaking out of a rut 63
8. For such a time as this 75
9. Learning to fly 85
10. Mountain-moving faith 96
11. True worship 106
12. The time is now! 116

1. CLOSE YOUR EYES AND SEE

The Latin phrase, *'Carpe diem'* literally translates to *'seize the day.'* The phrase comes from Book 1 of Roman poet Horace's *Odes*, written around 23 BC. In the original Latin, it's part of the longer phrase *'carpe diem, quam minimum credula postero,'* which translates to *'Seize the day, put very little trust in tomorrow.'*

So, whenever anyone exhorts us to *'seize the day,'* they are simply saying, *'Make the most of every opportunity you have right now!'* That is exactly what the Apostle Paul wrote to the Christians in Ephesus many years ago:

> **Ephesians 5:15-16** *"Be very careful, then, how you live – not as unwise but as wise, making the most of every opportunity, because the days are evil."*

As I was giving some thought and prayer to what might follow my last book on discipleship, a number of different issues and subjects came into my mind and so I began writing them down as headings. I stopped when I got to twelve and realised that in some ways, they were totally unrelated topics and didn't really form a normal book in the way we might expect.

But then that old Latin phrase just leapt from the page. *Carpe Diem; Seize the Day!* Each and every heading I had written down, represented a different way we could seize the day as we wrestled with each of those issues.

So, I had my next book, and I believe each of these twelve chapters will stand alone and speak to different people in different ways. But together, they will provide a valuable toolbox for those who really want to make the most of every opportunity, every day.

In this first chapter I want to give you a paradox, and the Oxford Dictionary defines that word the following way:

A paradox is a statement contrary to received opinion; A statement that, whether true or not, seems absurd at first hearing. A person, thing or statement conflicting with preconceived notions of the reasonable or possible.

The Bible is full of paradoxical statements and events. Things which don't make sense on the surface. Statements that appear to be contradictions or impossibilities. The most famous is the statement Jesus made in Matthew 10:39 when He said, *"Whoever finds his life will lose it, and whoever loses his life for my sake will find it."*

Well, I present you with another paradox today in the title of this chapter, as I encourage you to close your eyes and see. You already know that when you close your eyes, you see nothing. You shut out the world around you visually and you see only darkness. So, it doesn't make a lot of sense to suggest that we need to close our eyes to see, does it?

Such a statement seems like nonsense - just as nonsensical, I would suggest, as finding your life and losing it or losing your life and finding it - and yet that happens to be one of the most profound statements in the whole New Testament. So, allow me then to unpack this paradox a little more.

Today is the first day of the rest of your life. Today, like every day, is a fresh gift from God and a new beginning – or at least it can be a new beginning if you let it. Now in this new day, you have a choice in what you see when you look ahead. You can look at just another day; the same old same old; here we go again; the great clock of the universe has chimed once more as another day disappears, and a new one begins.

You can look with your physical eyes at a world that is not much different to the one you left behind yesterday. You can make judgements about yourself, your family, your job, your city, your church and even your God - based solely on what you see with your physical eyes.

I suggest this is how the majority of people, Christian or not, greet each new day. Alternatively, you can close your eyes and see - and I mean *really* see the world as it *actually* is.

I remember as a little boy having a vivid imagination and I would often close my eyes at all times of the day and night, to block out the reality of the human world around me for a while so I could go anywhere, do anything and be anyone I wanted to be.

Our imagination is an amazing thing, and I remember having such incredible adventures as I saw things that no one else could see. As a young boy I knew what it was like to close your eyes and see.

Of course, you can't continue living in this human world without opening your eyes again and being aware of the reality that is around you. That is important because you will end up flat on your face if you walk around all day with your eyes closed!

The sad fact is that when we grew up, most of us lost the ability or even the desire to close our eyes and see. Our childlike imagination and dreaming of another reality, gave way to the stark reality of what is around us each day. That is understandable, but tragic.

It is tragic to realise that there are people in our world today for whom the only reality that exists is that which they see with their physical eyes.

That is the finite, touch it, smell it, taste it, see it, hear it 'real' world around them. I am saddened when I encounter that in an unbeliever, but even more concerned to find it in so many Christians.

There are too many people who claim to be indwelt by the life of Jesus Christ who do not know how to close their eyes and see the wonderful and amazing world which the Bible calls the Kingdom of God or the Kingdom of Heaven.

As we sit here now there is a small 'r' reality which we can see and touch and articulate; we could describe the building we are in and the people who are around us; we could go on to describe our life, our calling and our career; we could speak about our family and our friends and our house and our car and our church and our city and our nation etc.

All these things we see and this is the reality we perceive when we look with our eyes. For far too many people, that is the *only* reality which exists – and let's be honest – in this broken, dysfunctional world, that is a pretty depressing reality most days!

However, for those pilgrims who are brave enough to close their eyes and see; for those believers who are willing to walk by faith and not by sight; for those who want to see a big "R" Reality - they can catch a glimpse of the *real* world; they can see what God sees and it is so much more detailed and so much more amazing than anything we could ever dream about.

Let me tell you a true story, which will illustrate what I mean. I am sure many of you may have already heard it – but it is a perfect illustration for us today. There were two men, both seriously ill, occupying the same hospital room.

One man was allowed to sit up in his bed for one hour each afternoon to help drain the fluid from his lungs and his bed was next to the room's only window.

The other man had to spend all his time flat on his back. The men talked for hours on end. They spoke about their wives and families; their homes; their jobs; their involvement in the military, where they had been on vacation etc. Then every afternoon when the man in the bed by the window could sit up for one hour, he would pass the time by describing to his roommate all the things he could see outside the window.

The man in the other bed began to live for that hour each day where his whole perspective on the world would be broadened and enlivened by all the activity and colour of the world outside. The man said the window overlooked a park with a lovely lake. Ducks and swans played on the water while children sailed their model boats. Young lovers walked arm in arm amidst flowers of every colour of the rainbow. Grand old trees graced the landscape, and a fine view of the city skyline could be seen in the distance.

As the man by the window described all this in exquisite detail, the man on the other side of the room would close his eyes as the picturesque scene became more and more real each day. One warm afternoon the man by the window described a parade passing by. Although the other man couldn't hear the band - he could see it in his mind's eye as the gentleman by the window portrayed it with beautiful and incredibly descriptive words.

Then unexpectedly, a sinister thought entered his mind. Why should this other man experience all the pleasures of seeing everything while he himself never got to see a thing? It didn't seem fair.

At first thought the man felt ashamed. But as the days passed and he missed seeing beyond the ceiling above his bed, his envy eroded into resentment and soon turned him sour. He began to brood, and he found himself unable to sleep. *'I should be next to that window!'* became the thought which now seemed to control his life.

Late one night as he lay staring at the ceiling, the man by the window began to cough. He was choking on the fluid in his lungs. The other man watched in the dimly lit room as the struggling man by the window groped for the button to call for help.

Listening from across the room he never moved, he never pushed his own button which would have brought the nurse running in. After five tense minutes, the coughing and choking stopped, along with the sound of breathing. Now there was only silence - deathly, cold silence.

The following morning the day-nurse arrived to check in on the two men. When she found the lifeless body of the man by the window, she was deeply saddened and called the hospital attendants to take him away.

As soon as it seemed appropriate, the other man asked if he could be moved next to the window. The nurse was happy to make the switch, and after making sure the man was comfortable, she left him alone.

Slowly and painfully, he propped himself up on one elbow to take his first look at the wonderful world outside which his former roommate had described so beautifully. Finally, he would have the joy of seeing it all himself. He strained to turn and look out the window, only to discover it faced a blank, old and dirty brick wall.

The man later asked the nurse what could have compelled his deceased roommate to describe such wonderful things outside this window. The nurse explained that the man was blind and could not see out the window either! She said, *"Perhaps he could see a world beyond his darkness and limitations, and maybe he just wanted to encourage you."*

Now I could preach ten sermons from that story, but there is one point I want to drive home as you begin to reflect on how you might seize the day; one question which I want to ask you today: What do you see out your window each day? Each of us has a window; each of us is looking out that window right now as I ask you what you can see?

What does 'the world according to you' look like? Do you just see that boring, predictable, lifeless brick wall just like the one you saw yesterday and last month and last year? Is it kind of like the wall in the prisoner's cell as he ticks off the days, months and years until his release? Is that what you see out your window?

I fear that for many people that is all they see. Or do you do what I try to still do? I am certainly not a little boy anymore, but I still know how to close my eyes and see. I mean what do you <u>really</u> see?

I am not talking about fairy stories or dreams with no substance; we may see them too, but I am talking about seeing with our spiritual eyes; seeing with God's eyes.

For example, when you look around you with human eyes at your church family, what do you see? Do you just see a collection of nice people who enjoy each other's company; who meet in a comfortable building each Sunday; sing some nice worship and praise songs; enjoy fellowship over a cuppa and some award-winning scones?

Do you see a church that looks and sounds like many other churches - nothing really to get too excited about? Let me tell you what I saw when I closed my eyes and really looked at my church family when I was writing this chapter.

Let me tell you what I really see. I see all those who worship with me every week and call my church their home. But I also see the many, many more who are being drawn by God and who will join us one day soon.

I see who and what my brothers and sisters are right now, but I also see what they are becoming. I see a group of people who have journeyed through some major valleys and enjoyed some breath-taking mountain views as well. I see people who have been tested through trials and have been found faithful.

I see people who have the power of God in them and who are being trained and equipped and readied so that God can issue the command to march across this city and lead thousands into the Kingdom of God as we go.

I see a church that is embracing a fresh understanding of God's grace in all its truth and that is releasing the true gospel in them which is going to spread throughout this city and this nation like a raging bushfire.

I see a vision which is so much more than words in a document, it's a living reality as people see their dreams fulfilled and as God's kingdom comes and God's will is done in our community as it is in heaven.

But then I see more … I see the dark side too. We cannot be selective in what we see when we close our eyes, it is all there and we need to see it all, in perspective. I see the plans of the devil and how he is so cleverly cutting across the purposes of God.

I see demons attacking the people of God through gossip and slander and laziness and bad theology and multiple distractions and a lack of loyalty and commitment to a local Church. I see people discouraged, doubting and despairing because they took their eyes off Jesus.

But then I see God. I see God as He really is and not as fallen humans have perceived Him or portrayed him ... and what a sight that is! I can feel the faith and the courage and the power and the determination to press on growing inside me as I behold our God ... as He really is.

He is the Lord Almighty, Omnipotent King, Lion of Judah, Rock of Ages, Prince of Peace, the King of Kings and the Lord of Lords, our Paternal Leader, Ruling Lord, the Reigning King of all the universe. He is my Father, He is my Helper, He is my Guardian, my Provider and Protector.

He is God. He is the First and Last, the Beginning and the End. He is the keeper of Creation and the Creator of all He keeps. He is the Architect of the universe and the Manager time. He is risen and brings power. He reigns and brings Peace.

He is the wisdom of the wise, He is the power of the powerful, He is the ancient of days, He is the ruler of rulers, He is the leader of leaders, He is the overseer of the overcomers, He is the sovereign Lord of all that was and is and is to come. He is light, love, longevity, and Lord. He is goodness, kindness, gentleness, and God.

He is Holy, Righteous, mighty, powerful, and pure. He is my redeemer, He is my saviour, He is my guide, He is my peace. He is my Joy, He is my comfort, He is my Lord. He always was, He always is, He always will be ... unmoved, unchanged, undefeated, never undone.

He was bruised and brought healing. He was pierced and eased pain. He was persecuted and brought freedom. He was dead and brought life.

The world can't understand Him. The armies can't defeat Him. The schools can't explain Him. The leaders can't ignore Him. The Pharisees couldn't confuse Him. The people can't control Him! The New Age can't replace Him. Herod couldn't kill Him. Nero couldn't crush Him. Hitler couldn't silence Him. Experts can't explain Him away! His ways are right. His word is eternal. His will is unchanging,

Then I see even more of this God ... I see that His mind is on me! His burden is light. His goal for me is abundant life. He rules my life. I serve Him because His bond is love. I follow Him because He is. He will never leave me. He will never forsake me. He will never mislead me. He will never forget me. He will never overlook me. He will never cancel my appointment in His appointment book!

When I fall, He lifts me up. When I fail, He forgives. When I'm weak, He is strong. When I'm lost, He is the way. When I am afraid, He is my courage. When I stumble, He steadies me. When I am hurt, He heals me. When I am broken, He mends me. When I am blind, He leads me.

When I am hungry, He feeds me. When I face trails, He is with me. When I face persecution, He strengthens me. When I face problems, He comforts me.

When I face loss, He provides for me. When I finally die, He will carry me home! He is everything for everybody, everywhere, every time, and in every way. He is God. He is faithful. I am His, and He is mine! God is in control. I am on His side, and that means all is well with my soul!

It really is amazing what you can see when you close your eyes for a moment and focus on the big 'R' reality as God sees it.

All through the Bible, from cover to cover; from Genesis to revelation; from Adam and Eve to the new heaven and new earth; we encounter men, women and young people who knew how to close their eyes and see!

What about Abraham: with human eyes he saw only the fact that he had lost the plot. He heard voices from an unknown God; packed up everything and left home; heading for nowhere.

He was the laughingstock of his hometown! But Abraham closed his eyes, and he could see his barren wife nursing his son; he could see a promised land so amazing, so wonderful that words could not express its beauty.

Abraham had a really tough journey, and he made a number of mistakes along the way, and he had some pretty discouraging experiences. But he only had to close his eyes and see what God was doing and where God was leading him – then Abraham could face another day; then Abraham could seize the day!

Moses closed his eyes and could no longer see a bunch of complaining, ungrateful people, but a land flowing with milk and honey.

Jesus closed His eyes in the Garden of Gethsemane that cold, lonely night and gradually the small 'r' reality which was dominated by pain and anguish of spirit and sorrow to the point of death faded as the big 'R' reality took over and for the joy set before him by His Father in the real world, Jesus got up and continued His journey to the cross.

What about you, now, today? What do you see? Is your sight limited to the temporal, material, human realm around you, or are you brave enough to close your eyes now and dream some dreams and see what is really happening in the spiritual realm and what God is doing right now and what God is promising to do in you and through you in the days ahead?

Do you really want to seize the day, or will you continue to let the day seize you?

It is my prayer that each and every one of us will have the courage, the commitment and the determination to close our eyes and see and then hear the words of the Apostle Paul once more:

> **1 Corinthians 2:9** *"No eye has seen, no ear has heard, no mind has conceived what God has prepared for those who love him ... but God has revealed it to us by his Spirit."*

So, close your eyes and see it ... then open your eyes and live it.

2. DEALING WITH THE PAST

Wouldn't it be wonderful if, by some miracle, we could begin again, knowing what we know now? Things would be different, wouldn't they? It is too bad life can't be lived in reverse, if that were the case, you could use some of that mature knowledge to avoid making the mistakes which you ultimately regret later. But that's not the way life works. In fact, I think we might need to make some mistakes in order to gain the knowledge, and we have all made our fair share of mistakes.

There have been many times in my life when things just didn't turn out right. During some of those times, I found myself wishing I could turn back the hands of time. I longed to be able to start all over!

I believe those times come to us all in our journey on earth. Some have made the wrong career choice and wish they could go back to school to be retrained, but now they must support a family. Some have made a bad business deal and now they are ruined and need to start from scratch again. How they wish they could go back. A failed marriage ruins family life and deeply wounds everyone involved. If only we could begin again and do it better.

These kinds of events occur every day and no one is exempt from them. Think of the things in your life that you would like the opportunity to change. Oh, how we would like a do-over sometimes.

We call these memories 'the past' for obvious reasons - these experiences are in the past because they have passed! So, it is obvious that you can't change them. What's done is done. The mistakes we have made are very real and sadly, so are the consequences.

But there is hope. The good news of the Gospel is that it is possible to begin again. There is forgiveness for the past in Christ. That's the good news. But there is some bad news which comes with the good news. Sadly, there are many who have received this forgiveness, but they still seem plagued by the past.

One of the greatest obstacles facing those of us who want to truly 'seize the day' today ... is yesterday! The past can be like a ball and chain around our ankles as we try to take strides towards the new day. Until we learn to deal with the past, we will never be able to seize the day and make the most of the opportunities we are given today.

For most of us, the past holds many good memories. We remember the good times: times when we were happy and enjoying life; times when we were with someone special. We remember the special events: birthdays, graduations, weddings and anniversaries, the birth of children and grandchildren.

Good memories are a wonderful thing. It's great to be able to tune in and play them back. It brings a smile to our face. We can certainly thank God for the good memories.

The past can also give us valuable perspective. Although it has been said that *"the only thing we learn from the past is that we don't learn from the past"* ... we can actually learn from the past. If we let it, the past can teach us many things about living in the present.

The past is like the rearview mirror in our car. As we move forward, we regularly glance at it to keep us aware of what is behind us. The past makes us more knowledgeable and wiser. In that regard, the past is very good.

But the past also has a powerful dark side. The past can become a prison. It's possible for the past to put us in a deep bondage. Along with the good memories, there are the memories of failure. Sometimes our memory can haunt us and debilitate us. Our failures can cause us to see ourselves as failures, or as unable to break the patterns of failure in our lives. We often stereotype ourselves and thereby put ourselves in bondage. Many people live today imprisoned by their past – just where the devil wants them.

In the most extreme cases, we see people sitting in mental hospitals constantly reliving the tragic events of yesterday. They are trapped by the things that have been and can't see the things that are and could be.

So how do we deal with the past? Some people re-live the past. They recount all the events of the past in great detail in their minds, over and over again. All of those negative emotions which they felt back then, they feel again. They beat themselves up because of experiences that are forever gone and will never change.

Some people end up surrendering to the past. They decide that they will never rise above the past, so they resign themselves to be what the past has made them. After all, the lot has been cast, and they are now the product of their past.

Others learn how to defy the effect of the past and refuse to be dominated by what has happened before today. They recognise that while the past is an unchangeable part of their history, they can do something about the impact of the past on them today. They can't control what has already happened, but they can control how they deal with the memories of the past. This is the key to how we deal with the past. There are basically three things you must do to effectively conquer your past, so you can seize the day.

The first is that you must recognise the past for what it is, the past. It is over, done, gone, finished, ended, it has passed. You can't change one single thing that happened back then, whether back then was years ago or yesterday.

The second thing that you must do is recognise Satan's strategy in reminding you of the past. His strategy is to discourage you and defeat you and the easiest way to do that for many people is to trap them in their past.

The third thing you must understand is that you have complete control over the impact of the past on your life today. While you can't change what has happened, you can change the way you respond to what has happened. Simply put, we need divine amnesia.

Forget the past ...

The Apostle Paul tells us that the way to deal with the past is to forget it.

> **Philippians 3:13-14** *"Brothers and sisters, I do not consider myself yet to have taken hold of it. But one thing I do: Forgetting what is behind and straining toward what is ahead, I press on toward the goal to win the prize for which God has called me heavenward in Christ Jesus."*

Paul is saying that the way to deal with the past is to forget it. We need divine amnesia. We know what amnesia is, but divine amnesia is something only God can give us. When I speak about forgetting the past, of course, I'm not talking about forgetting it mentally. Although there are many things I wish I could forget, unfortunately, God created our minds to be incredibly powerful. Even though we might not remember something consciously, sub-consciously it is always there.

Every act, word, event, situation and circumstance is imbedded forever in our minds. When Paul speaks about forgetting the past, he means that we must forget it in the sense that we no longer allow it to have any control in our lives. Unless we learn to forget the past in this sense, we will always be on a leash. We will attempt to move forward in life, only to be snatched back time and again.

If you are thinking, *"Well, that's easier said than done,"* you are right. But, by God's grace, it can be done. Christ can liberate us from the past. The reason Christ came to this earth was to offer His life on the cross so that our sins might be forgiven. Christ can forgive our past.

The Bible teaches that Jesus Christ can release us from sin and the guilt of sin. There is nothing in your past too great for God to handle; no sin too big for God to forgive; no mistake too great that He cannot empower us to move on from it. Christ can enable and empower us to release the past and consciously embrace the present. He can enable us to replace what has been with what can be. He can truly empower us to seize the day!

Be intentional in the present ...

We must not only develop a divine amnesia in terms of forgetting the past; but we must also engage in a deliberate activity in the present. To deal with the past effectively, we must live in the present and be intentional.

One of the important keys to truly living in the present is replacing pessimism from the past with optimism. It's very hard to face failure in your own personal life and come away with an optimistic attitude. Pessimism seems to reign, and pessimism creates a cycle of despair.

Many times, we become locked into pessimistic ways of thinking, and we end up bound mentally by these patterns of thought. Past failures may suggest to us that we will never succeed. After all, we have tried and failed. But often that is not the reality of the situation.

There was an experiment done with the Great Northern Pike fish in America years ago. The fish were placed into a tank with their favourite food, minnows. The problem was that a glass divider was inserted into the tank between the Pike and the minnows. Every time the Pike went for the minnows, they bumped their noses into this glass divider.

Finally, convinced that the minnows were beyond reach, the fish simply gave up trying. When the glass divider was removed, the Great Northern Pike did not go for even one minnow. Sometimes, we are like those fish. We've been convinced that we could never break free from the patterns of defeat and failure that have bound us. But that is not true.

God is an eternal optimist. I know that because when Jesus ascended into heaven, He put His disciples in charge of winning the world. But we can be optimists, too. We can be optimists when we come to understand that God truly has a plan for our lives. We can begin to look to the future with hope. A divine expectation can be created and grow within our hearts. An anticipation of what the possibilities are for our life can replace all those negative patterns of thought which have bound us for so long.

If we are to live successfully in the present, we must not only put the past aside, but we must replace pessimism with optimism. There are good things which lie ahead. Say that to yourself every day, every hour is if you need to ... there are good things which lie ahead.

Not only must we replace pessimism with optimism, but we must also replace passivism with activism. The past seeks to trap us by discouraging us to the point where we are so mentally exhausted, we just don't want to try any more. Depressed people don't even like to get out of bed and when they do, they just sit around in their pyjamas all day long or engage in hours of mind-numbing television or social media scrolling.

Sometimes the first step out of that situation is to get out of bed, put your clothes on and do something useful! We need to act in faith and truly believe in what God can do. Paul says that he *reaches towards what lies ahead.* He is someone who is involved with the living of life. He is not merely content to be acted upon. He must act himself, and if we are to succeed, we must act as well.

I have said many times that it's impossible to steer a parked car. Parked cars go nowhere. You can turn the steering wheel all you like, but it doesn't change anything. Only as we begin to move, are we able to accomplish those things we would like to see come to pass. We must be active. We must be on the move before God can guide us.

Jesus calls us to follow Him – not sit and watch Him pass by! The Christian life is a commitment to *do* something as well as *be* someone. The Christian life has been likened to a walk, a race, a fight. Those are all action terms. When Jesus calls us, He calls us not just to believe in Him intellectually, but to follow Him in the living of our lives.

It's possible for a person to believe in Jesus intellectually like he believes in Napoleon or George Washington. You can hold an intellectual belief without making a commitment to it. But that is not biblical faith. Faith in Jesus means we put our trust in Him. We trust Him with our very lives.

As we commit ourselves to follow Him and live for Him each and every day. The Apostle Paul said he was reaching forward towards that which lies ahead. The picture here is of someone who is stretching forward, like a runner in a race, seeking to win, not merely to finish. But if we would win over the past, we must also be willing to aggressively stretch forward – not look back!

Be determined in reaching forward ...

Now we must take willingness one step further. As we stretch forward, we really must possess the quality of a determined attitude.

Look again at the words of the Apostle Paul, "*One thing I do: forgetting what lies behind and reaching forward to what lies ahead, I press on toward the goal for the prize of the upward call of God in Christ Jesus.*"

Here is a man who is not content with just being willing. He is not simply reaching forward to what lies ahead, he is giving his all to that endeavour. He is so determined in his attitude that nothing will deter him.

We must have this same determined attitude if we would succeed in conquering the demons of the past. We need to understand that we are engaged in real warfare. To be plagued by the past is to be under spiritual attack. That is why we must counter-attack by employing a strategy like Paul's, whereby we forget the past and actively focus on the future.

Perhaps a closing thought on how to do this from the life of Jehoshaphat would help us understand what this determined attitude looks like. In 2 Chronicles 20 we find Jehoshaphat, King of Israel, in big trouble.

He had three enemy nations preparing to attack him and He was completely outnumbered and overwhelmed, in human terms. We can apply the principles he applied to the enemy of the bondage of the past. Jehoshaphat did five really important things.

1. He identified the enemy. We must recognise that there is a real and present force behind the negative emotions we feel from past events.

2. He took it to the Lord. In verses 3-4 he proclaims a fast in order to seek help from the Lord.

3. He admitted his inadequacy. Jehoshaphat, speaking to God, said in verse 12, "… *we have no power to face this vast army that is attacking us. We do not know what to do, but our eyes are on you.*"

4. He turned his attention to God.

5. He relaxed in faith. God spoke to Jehoshaphat in verse 15 and said, "*Do not be afraid or discouraged because of this vast army. For the battle is not yours, but God's.*" In other words, God was saying to quit struggling and just relax.

Sometimes we are tempted to work things out for ourselves. When we fail, we feel that we have disappointed God. We feel that we have let God down. But we cannot let God down because we don't hold God up. He holds us up. We don't have God in our hands. He has us in His hands.

What God wants us to do is to allow Him to work through us. If you relax in faith, God will enable you to forget the past, engage with the present and look to the future. Then, and only then, will you be able to truly seize the day!

3. ARE YOU CONNECTED?

Are You connected? That's a question that matters these days - at least as far as your success out in the world is concerned. Do you know the right people? Have you made the right contacts? Have you nurtured friendships with people in high places? Are you networked? Are you online? When was the last time you checked your e-mail or social media accounts? If the rich, famous, and important come knocking at your door or calling online today, will you be ready to answer? Are you connected?

It's true that the people who are 'connected' in this way are the ones who are often deemed successful and important - both in the world and even in the church. How many times have you heard it said, or implied, at least, that the people who are most desirable for leadership roles in the church are the ones who've achieved great things in the secular world? Who wouldn't want a church leadership full of doctors, lawyers, senators, and top executives? And how do you achieve success in those realms, if not by consciously connecting with the powerful, the respectable, and the generous?

It's true in every area of twenty first century life in our nation and others, the church included: We are driven to devote energy to relationships with particular groups of people, and we are equally driven to avoid getting bogged down in relationships with other, less desirable, or less important groups of people. Yet the claims of the gospel make it incredibly clear that there is much more to human relationships than that. In fact, the gospel in many places goes directly against this benchmark of modern culture which says that the most important thing in life is who you know, and how well you know them.

The events and news of our world are often punctuated by stories, some fictional, some real, of people who've realised that - even though 'being connected' to other people is an absolutely vital part of life - there is indeed more to 'being connected' with others than simply calculating what they can give back to us in return.

In the 1988 movie Rain Man, Tom Cruise plays a somewhat greedy, self-centred fellow who's initially trying to figure out a way to get the whole of the family inheritance away from his brother Raymond, played by Dustin Hoffman. Raymond is an autistic savant, which means that, although his intellect is top-level, far above the average, his social skills and his ability to interact in the world are severely lacking. So his brother is determined to convince Raymond and all other interested parties that the family money is worth nothing to Raymond, but it could definitely be worth something to him!

So, this 'connects' with his special-needs brother, for the sole purpose of getting something back for his efforts. Over the course of the movie, though, the greedy brother realizes that there's more to his relationship with Raymond, after all, than simply getting the money away from him. There's the simple joy of being in a relationship with another person, a joy that I gradually intensified for him by the growing knowledge that Raymond can never truly repay what he's doing for him. There is more to 'being connected' to others than the simple calculation of what they can give back to us in return!

This lesson was also learned by former US President, Jimmy Carter. As a career politician, Carter endured many years of the obligatory 'superficial connections' which always characterize political campaigning.

These connections and so-called friendships are usually only entered with a view to a payoff, a profit gained out of the relationship.

After his time as President, though, Jimmy Carter turned his efforts to humanitarian work; in his final years he devoted a great deal of time to building homes for needy families through Habitat for Humanity.

He, too, realized - in his case, as a result of his Christian faith - that there's great joy to be found in entering into a relationship and doing meaningful things for other people who can never possibly pay you back for your efforts.

Jesus teaches us this lesson so well. He taught it through His actions - by entering into a life-changing relationship with the Samaritan woman at the well in John 4, knowing full well the life history of that woman and knowing that His consorting with her would do nothing for His own reputation; by performing miraculous healings of so many needy men and women, knowing that they could never truly repay him for his deeds; and ultimately, by suffering a sacrificial, substitutionary death at Calvary, entering a relationship with us by providing a gift that not even the sum total of all human goodness from now until eternity could ever repay.

Jesus calls each of us to relate to others in a way that pays no attention to status - neither our own status nor the status of the other person. For example:

> **Luke 14:1, 7-14** *"One Sabbath, when Jesus went to eat in the house of a prominent Pharisee, he was being carefully watched. ... When he noticed how the guests picked the places of honour at the table, he told them this parable:*

"When someone invites you to a wedding feast, do not take the place of honour, for a person more distinguished than you may have been invited. If so, the host who invited both of you will come and say to you, 'Give this person your seat.' Then, humiliated, you will have to take the least important place.

But when you are invited, take the lowest place, so that when your host comes, he will say to you, 'Friend, move up to a better place.' Then you will be honoured in the presence of all the other guests. For all those who exalt themselves will be humbled, and those who humble themselves will be exalted."

Then Jesus said to his host, "When you give a luncheon or dinner, do not invite your friends, your brothers or sisters, your relatives, or your rich neighbours; if you do, they may invite you back and so you will be repaid. But when you give a banquet, invite the poor, the crippled, the lame, the blind, and you will be blessed. Although they cannot repay you, you will be repaid at the resurrection of the righteous."

Stories like that one from Jesus make very clear the truth that it's not who you know; it's simply how well you're willing to get to know them, and how much of yourself you're willing to give in the process. What drives us to pursue certain relationships, and ignore others?

There is certain behaviour in that regard mandated by the world; but there's also relational behaviour that's mandated by the Kingdom of God. Whether you realize it or not, you answer the question every day: To whom will you cater? Who will be the focus of your energy? The world's agenda - which Jesus warns against in this passage - tells us to cater to fame, fortune, and family.

In verse 8, there's reference to a 'distinguished' guest who is so important in the world's eyes - there's fame. And in verse 12 there's reference to the 'rich neighbours' - there's fortune. And these are the two biggies! We are taught from an early age, it seems, that we must find ways, if we hope to succeed, to woo the influential, and count ourselves in their ranks!

The third group here is family; this group is referred to in verse 12 as 'friends, brothers or sisters, relatives' - and the idea here is somewhat different, family is not necessarily influential; but the driving force here once again is status. You relate to that other person, give of yourself, only if you're dead sure that you'll get something back!

Do everything in your power to get yourself on equal footing with those who have fame and fortune. If you can't do that, then at least direct your effort towards family and friends, because you know where to find them whenever you need a favour or some kind of payback.

First, consider the Guest...

There are two distinct warnings that Jesus gives here; he does it by talking about two separate people, the guest and the host at the party. The first person Jesus directs our attention toward is the guest who arrives and immediately helps himself to the seat of greatest honour. Why does the guest do that? It's very simple:

The first step toward becoming a part of the in-group is acting and looking like a member of that group. Crash enough parties, take the seat of honour enough times, and pretty soon people will be convinced that you are a genuine 'honoured guest' and they'll start treating you as such.

You want to be a part of a certain group: the rich group here, the newsworthy group there, the powerful group over here, the group that seems to have the most fun. You know as well as the next person that the first step is to transform yourself to look, act, and talk like that group, then move into position to rub elbows with them, and voila! You're in.

Jesus says here: *Don't do it!* Why not? He tells the story of another guest coming in, this one is really and truly a distinguished guest; and he goes up to you and knocks you right out of the seat that you've claimed for yourself. In other words, Jesus says when you pretend to be something you're not to get 'connected' with this group or that, your position there is never as secure as you'd like to think!

You're never truly 'connected' to those folks in the way God intended for us to be connected to other people, because you've gone about it in the wrong way. And in general, the warning Jesus gives to us here is this: If you have to pretend to be something you're not in order to get someplace, you're better off not going. You're better off not going because, like the guest at the party, you've made 'connections' that are not genuinely secure in Christ.

Now, back to our original statement: "*Jesus calls us to connect to other people in a way that pays no attention to status.*" How well are you living that out?

A word of warning: if in your relationships with others you find yourself ever mindful of your own status, and often pretending to be something that you're not, masquerading as more powerful, more intelligent, more worldly, more willing to compromise your values than you should, then status is an issue - your own and the other person's - and you're not making the unconditional connections with other people that Jesus intended.

Jesus' first warning, then, centres around the guest. A second warning that Jesus gives in the passage relates to the host of the party. The host is the one who went all out to invite the famous, the fortunate, and the familiar to the party in the first place. And Jesus' warning once again is, *don't do it!* Why not? He says, because it points squarely to the fact that the host is only inviting those people who can repay him in some way. His motives are self-serving.

Second, consider the Host

Jesus gives us this second warning: If you must expect a reward for doing something, you're better off not doing it. You're better off not doing it because, once again, you're making connections that aren't genuinely secure in Christ. How well are you living up to Jesus' exhortation that we relate to other persons in a way that is not mindful of their status or our own?

This second warning is very clear: if I only exert myself to 'do' for others after careful consideration of what they can 'do in return' for me, then I've not met them on the unconditional ground of Christ, but rather I've connected with them because of their status. Whether it's fame, or fortune, or family; somehow, I've sized up the other person and said, "*Hey, there's someone who will come in handy one day. I better latch onto them.*" And once again, we have failed to make the kind of absolutely unconditional connections that Jesus expects us to make.

Fame. fortune. family. There's nothing wrong with these things; and Jesus is certainly not suggesting that we ignore these groups as we do the work of God's kingdom. However, we have overstepped when we use these things as required characteristics of all those to whom we might possibly reach out.

Jesus calls us to look beyond these marks of status and be willing to relate to, connect with, anyone whom God might lay in our path. In particular, Jesus insists in this story that we look specifically to those in the world who have no status! Jesus calls both the guest and the host to consider the fallen, the fearsome, and the famished. Who are these people?

The fallen ... are those with a past, those whose own status has taken a deathblow because of mistakes they've made. Like the woman at the well in John 4 who had a history of failed marriages and was shunned as a result – she was the one Jesus spent time with. Like the thief on the cross that Jesus invited into paradise. Like men and women in your own community who have things in their past that so many churches unfortunately treat like unforgivable sins - divorce, substance abuse, crime, sexual sins etc. Jesus calls you to connect with these people too when you have the opportunity.

It doesn't mean you condone actions that are indeed sinful; but it does mean that you don't let another person's status prevent you from reaching out to them; it means that you don't slink around hoping no one sees you, but rather you 'connect with' them unconditionally, because that's what Jesus calls us to do. Do you know anyone who's 'fallen'? People who aren't welcome in most people's lives? Let your life be the wedding banquet that 'rolls out the red carpet' for them.

The fearsome ... are those people who most of the world thinks are just a little bit scary; and we'd rather keep our distance from them, not because of anything they've done, but simply because of who they are, usually because of who they are on the outside. Jesus gives a rundown in verse 13: *the poor, the crippled, the lame, the blind.*

Who are the ones who are 'fearsome' in your community, in your life? The very poor, perhaps. Those of another skin colour, or of another nationality. Those who, I'm sure, are very good and respectable 'for their kind' (a phrase that God hates), but who just don't belong where 'I am.'

Jesus says that these are precisely the people that God's people are to connect with! People who aren't going to hear it anywhere else if you aren't willing to tell it to them. People who aren't going to know the love of God anywhere else if you aren't willing to let God love them through you. The fearsome.

The famished ... are people at the greatest possible point of need. The homeless; the jobless; those who are undergoing a great crisis. People who are all right, maybe just like me, that I'd like to deal with under normal circumstances, but right now they've got messes in their lives that I'd rather not get involved in.

Once again, Jesus says loud and clear: Get in there! Stop looking at the status of the other person; stop sizing up how much it's going to cost you, and how much they can give you back, and just get in there, and be God's messenger in a delicate, crucial situation.

There is someone out there on the fringe of your life today, that if you were to go to them and simply connect with them, one human being to another, it would be the greatest thing in their life. It would indeed be the equivalent to them of being invited to a great wedding banquet.

Be warned: They probably won't be able to pay you back. They may not be able to do anything for you in return. And you may not even get a pat on the back for your efforts.

But there's no greater joy in the Kingdom of God than to be able to relate to other people, meet them where they are, without being worried to death about what they can give back to you. And there's no greater joy in heaven than for God to see you and me doing just that, loving others unconditionally, networking unconditionally, without regard to status, fame, fortune, familiarity or anything else.

To truly seize the day, every day, we have to be prepared to make the most of every opportunity God provides for us to live an authentic Christian life. Seizing the day sounds like a selfish pursuit.

But as disciples of Jesus Christ, seizing the day means seizing the day <u>Jesus</u> gives us. Knowing His heart and His mission like we do, we should therefore assume that when we truly seize the day, it will more often than not involve us in connecting with and serving the needs of someone other than ourselves.

Just think about Jesus when He was walking among us all those years ago, how many hours in the day did he spend serving others, giving to others, blessing others, relating to others ... and how many hours of the day did He spend attending to His own personal needs?

That's what truly seizing the day looks like. Jesus showed us how. Are we prepared to follow Him wherever He leads us and seize day that He has made for us – not the one we planned?

May God open the eyes of our heart to hear His Word this day and receive it.

4. A NATION IN DECLINE

I was not a history student in high school. I couldn't see the point in looking backwards, I wanted to be a history maker with his eyes fixed on the horizon of new opportunities! How naïve I was; and how I wasted those years and failed to understand how important it is to learn from the past. Ironically, my first lecture in Bible college was Church History and I remember sighing inwardly and thinking, *"How boring this will be, let's get on with mission and ministry and all the saving-the-world stuff."*

I was 30 years old and still hadn't worked it out. But Dr Roger Kemp healed me of my ignorance in those lectures, week by week, as he unlocked the past and opened my eyes to the simple truth that history is one of our greatest teachers and the source of many of our most important lessons in life. It would be wrong to say that I became a history buff after that, but I do believe I am far more interested in understanding the past now, before trying to shape the future.

Ancient history was even more boring than modern history when I was young, but more recently, as I have looked back across the ruins and landmarks of antiquity, I have been stunned by the parallels between those societies and our own.

For most of us, the destruction of Carthage, the rise of the Greek city-states, and the Fall of Rome are just ghosts of the past, history lessons long forgotten (or slept through in my case). Such realities as the capture of Constantinople, the dissolution of the Holy Roman Empire, the collapse of the kingdoms of France and Spain, and the slow withering decline of the British Empire are much less clear and less memorable.

Most of us do not remember much from our history lessons about the French Enlightenment or the issues that led to the American Revolution. But it is vital that we reconsider the nature of life in those earlier times. For within those eras and movements are the seeds of the troubles we face today across all cultures.

There are many reasons for the decline and fall of a nation, but an important (and often overlooked) reason is its abandonment of faith. The roots of 'culture' come from the word 'cult.' In other words, culture (cult-ure) is based upon some form of religious or spiritual worldview. Egypt was a religious society founded on the worship of nature gods and goddesses. Greece and Rome had their pantheon of pagan deities. And nations like India, China, and many other parts of the globe all demonstrate the principle that civilization arises from a spiritual reality.

The opposite is also true. When the traditional beliefs of a nation erode, the nation dies. Our faith provides the set of standards that govern a nation. Historian Will Durant said, "*There is no significant example in history, before our time, of a society successfully maintaining moral life without the aid of religious faith.*"

Unfortunately, this great nation of ours has embarked on a journey to maintain a society without any spiritual foundation. Christian principles are no longer taught in the public schools like they once were and are often ridiculed in the arenas of education and media. One has to wonder what the fate of this country will be in the future. I believe Australia is still the greatest country in the world; I would not want to live anywhere else; but the naivety and ignorance which suggests it will always be that way must be challenged.

We are witnessing decay in our nation at almost every level: socially, culturally and morally. Those who have studied nations and civilisations in the past which have crumbled and disappeared, have witnessed the same patterns.

Social Decay

Three important trends demonstrate social decay. They are the crisis of lawlessness, loss of economic discipline and a rising bureaucracy. History provides ample illustrations of the disastrous consequences of the collapse of law and order. In ancient Greece, the first symptoms of disorder were a loss of respect for tradition and the degradation of the young. Among the early symptoms was the decline of art and entertainment. The philosophers distorted the medium of communication. Rhetoric became combative and intolerant; intellectuals began to deride and attack all the traditional institutions of Hellenic society. New thinkers in the society argued for 'fundamental change' and called for giving the youth a 'voice in society.'

Without traditional guidelines, the young men grew wild and undisciplined, quickly destroying the old order. Slowly Greece devolved into a disreputable and lawless nation. The Romans conquered Greece in 146 B.C. By placing everything under military authority, they were able to restore order and bring back the rule of law.

In a study of the French Revolution, one historian noted that *"Order is not pressure which is imposed on society from without, but an equilibrium which is set up from within."*

With regard to 'a lack of economic discipline' ... we are seeing this in the state of NSW in a big way ... we have seen it at the federal level in recent years and could well see that increase substantially following the outcome of the most recent federal election.

We have also seen a huge rise in bureaucracy in our nation over recent years. Apart from the enormous cost to the taxpayer, this has resulted in a gradual watering down of the decisive leadership required by Governments, especially during hard times or when our nation is under threat. The 'red tape', as they call it, can completely strangle a nation. When you study many other civilisations and societies in the past, you see that social decay led to their decline and ultimate fall. If we are to prevent a repeat of history, then we must learn from these lessons of history.

Cultural Decay

Four important trends demonstrate cultural decay. They are the 'decline of education,' the 'weakening of cultural foundations,' the 'loss of respect for tradition,' and the 'increase in materialism.' In his study The Civilization of Rome, Donald Dudley says that no single cause, by itself, would have brought that mighty empire to its knees. Instead, the fall came through "*a number of weaknesses in Roman society; their effects may be variously estimated, but in combination they must have been largely responsible for the collapse.*"

The cultural decay of a nation leads to social and cultural decline. And the patterns are similar from one civilization to another. Despite the great difference in cultural background - most of the ancient empires have shown very similar characteristics, and these characteristics provide the key to an understanding of the processes of their decline.

The Roman poet Livy wrote that greed and self-indulgence led Romans to dangerous excesses. He said, "*When people had fewer possessions, they were also modest in their desires. Riches brought avarice and abundant pleasures, and the desire to carry luxury and lust to the point of ruin.*"

In describing the decadence of the Roman Republic, one historian wrote that this preoccupation with luxury led to carnal indulgences. *"For some young men indulged in affairs with boys, others in affairs with courtesans."* They paid a talent (roughly a thousand dollars) for a boy bought for sexual pleasure and three hundred drachmas for a jar of caviar. Marcus Cato was outraged by this and, in a speech to the people at that time, he complained that one might be quite convinced of the decline of the republic, when pretty boys cost more than fields and jars of caviar cost more than workers in the field.

As we look at our society today, we too find ourselves in a world where values have been inverted and where citizens pursue selfish pleasures without counting the cost. Our nation would be wise to learn the lessons of the past.

Moral Decay

Three important trends demonstrate moral decay. They are the 'rise in immorality,' the 'decay of religious belief,' and the 'devaluing of human life.'

The classic study of Roman civilization, The Decline and Fall of the Roman Empire, written by English historian Edward Gibbon was published in 1776. He observed that the leaders of the empire gave into the vices of strangers, morals collapsed, laws became oppressive, and the abuse of power made the nation vulnerable to the barbarian hordes.

British historian Catherine Edwards demonstrated that our current examples of immorality are not a modern phenomenon. In her study of the 'politics of immorality' in ancient Rome, she says that contraception, abortion, and exposure were common ways to prevent childbirth in Rome.

Husbands refused to recognize any child they did not believe to be their own. Until accepted by its father, a Roman baby did not exist, legally speaking.

Life became cheap in the latter days of the Roman Empire. Burdensome regulation and taxes made manufacturing and trade unprofitable. Families were locked into hereditary trades and vocations allowing little if any vocational choice. Eventually, children were seen as a needless burden and abortion and infanticide became commonplace. In some cases, children were sold into slavery. Manners and social life fell into debauchery.

Under Justinian, entertainment grew bawdier and more bizarre. Orgies and love feasts were also very common. Homosexuality and bestiality were openly practiced. Under Nero, Christians were blamed for the great fire in Rome and horribly persecuted. Similar patterns can be found in other civilizations. In Greece, the music of the young people became wild and coarse. Popular entertainment was brutal and vulgar. Promiscuity, homosexuality, and drunkenness became a daily part of life. And all moral and social restraints were lost leading to greater decadence.

The parallels to our own nation are striking. No, we don't sacrifice infants to a pagan goddess, but we do sacrifice 80,000 unborn children every year on the altar of convenience. And various sexual practices are now openly accepted as part of an alternative lifestyle.

Are we a nation in decline?

A study of previous nations and civilisations reveal patterns of decline. Do these patterns apply to our own nation? Many people looking at the patterns of social, cultural, and moral decay in other countries and civilizations have concluded that we are headed down the same path.

Historian, Russell Kirk put it this way: *"It appears to me that our culture labours in an advanced state of decadence; that what many people mistake for the triumph of our civilization actually consists of powers that are disintegrating our culture; that the much praised 'democratic freedom' of liberal society in reality is servitude to appetites and illusions which attack religious belief; which destroy community through excessive centralization and urbanization; and which destroy life-giving tradition and custom."*

We as a nation and a people must rise to the occasion or suffer a fate similar to that which has befallen civilizations in the past. The task is not easy since the patterns of decay found in other nations strike ours as well.

Nations were subverted by false and foreign ideologies. We too find hostile ideas in the public arenas of media, politics, and education. Sexual promiscuity led to the downfall of these nations. So too we find similar patterns of sexual promiscuity and debauchery.

As nations fell into decline, life became cheap. Infants were strangled, exposed to the elements, or sold into slavery. Others were sacrificed to pagan goddesses in order to ensure productivity or a long life. Today life has become cheap. At one end of the spectrum, over 200 unborn babies are aborted every day in our nation. At the other end, physician-assisted suicide is becoming the norm for the aged.

Throughout history, in every culture and society there is a pattern of 'challenge and response.' We as a nation are challenged in fundamental ways, and our response will either pull us back from the brink or push us over it. Will we follow the path to renewal and reformation, or will we follow the path to destruction?

The choice is ours. The church as an institution in our society is now powerless. Jesus said He would build a church that the gates of hell itself would not prevail against. Look around people - hell is prevailing against the church of this age. We are having the heaven kicked out of us every single day in a myriad of ways!

The visible church - the established, man-made institution which consists of buildings, programs, clergy & lay people; that identifiable people group within society who do culturally irrelevant things on Sundays and Wednesday nights; is marginalised, irrelevant and shrinking in size and proportion every day.

But Jesus said, *"I will build a church that kicks Satan's butt all the way to hell!"* (My paraphrase). So where is that church? How will it be built? How long must we watch our nation decline and decay in front of our eyes before the church that Jesus promised to build emerges? I am so glad you asked. I have some good news for you. I know you were hoping there was some good news somewhere in this sermon, weren't you? Well, there is. Jesus is building His church. He never stopped. Little by little His Spirit is changing the mindset of believers across this nation and mobilising them one by one to infiltrate the world and turn society on its head, the way the early church did all those years ago!

The church-building strategies of Jesus are not new - they are as old as the church itself. He showed us over 2,000 years ago and He even wrote it down in the Bible so we wouldn't forget it. Jesus came into the midst of our human society and from within that society He manifested the Kingdom of God. He was the ultimate 'incarnational' minister. He was the master of 'infiltration.' He was the original 'lifestyle evangelism' trainer.

He did not come and show us how to erect buildings to hide in; or run programs which don't mean anything to the world around us. He showed us how to live out our faith in the midst of a hostile world.

church leaders are no longer respected in our nation. Sex scandals and the rapidly declining moral fibre within denominational leaders has seen a once respected and valued institution slip very quickly into disrepute. The church is ridiculed by many and ignored by even more.

So there is only one way Jesus can still be salt and light in this nation, by doing what He did in the first place and what He showed us to do: incarnational ministry ... infiltrating society at every level and bringing salt and light to the roots of our society ... rather than trying to bring it to the distant edges of our culture where nobody notices. We need to get out of the grandstands and back into the game!

Wherever there is a place in which we can shine the light of God, we must take the opportunity. Not as Bible-bashing Christians talking a language that people don't understand, but as plumbers, lawyers, builders, housewives, managers, mothers, fathers, grandparents, nurses, teachers, doctors, tradespeople, politicians etc. Infiltration and incarnation.

That is how Jesus is building His church. That is the only way He can now, in a society which no longer holds the institutionalised church in high esteem. Perhaps it was the only way He ever wanted to build His church in the first place?

If we are serious about fulfilling God's will in this city and this nation, if we truly want to seize the day and take hold of the opportunities God has given us ... then there will be no more spectators.

No more sideline commentators. We are _all_ called into the church-building business, in partnership with the Master Builder Himself. None of us get to watch from a distance, we must get dirty on the field, playing our part, however small it appears, in the master plan of God to restore righteousness in this nation.

Come, Holy Spirit, fill us afresh and give us the courage to seize the day, today, and bring this mighty nation back from the brink and restore our spiritual foundations!

5. HAVE YOU SEEN JESUS?

John 1:14-18, 29, 35-52 *"The Word became flesh and made his dwelling among us. We have seen his glory, the glory of the One and Only, who came from the Father, full of grace and truth. John testifies concerning him. He cries out, saying, "This was he of whom I said, 'He who comes after me has surpassed me because he was before me.'"*

From the fullness of his grace we have all received one blessing after another. For the law was given through Moses; grace and truth came through Jesus Christ. No one has ever seen God, but God the One and Only, who is at the Father's side, has made him known

The next day John saw Jesus coming toward him and said, "Behold, the Lamb of God, who takes away the sin of the world! This is the one I meant when I said, 'A man who comes after me has surpassed me because he was before me.'

The next day John was there again with two of his disciples. When he saw Jesus passing by, he said, "Look, the Lamb of God!" When the two disciples heard him say this, they followed Jesus. Turning around, Jesus saw them following and asked, "What do you want?" They said, "Rabbi" (which means Teacher), "where are you staying?" "Come," he replied, "and you will see."

So they went and saw where he was staying and spent that day with him. It was about the tenth hour. Andrew, Simon Peter's brother, was one of the two who heard what John had said and who had followed Jesus.

The first thing Andrew did was to find his brother Simon and tell him, "We have found the Messiah" (that is, the Christ).

And he brought him to Jesus. Jesus looked at him and said, "You are Simon son of John. You will be called Cephas" (which, when translated, is Peter).

The next day Jesus decided to leave for Galilee. Finding Philip, he said to him, "Follow me." Philip, like Andrew and Peter, was from the town of Bethsaida. Philip found Nathanael and told him, "We have found the one Moses wrote about in the Law, and about whom the prophets also wrote - Jesus of Nazareth, the son of Joseph." "Nazareth! Can anything good come from there?" Nathanael asked. "Come and see," said Philip.

When Jesus saw Nathanael approaching, he said of him, "Here is a true Israelite, in whom there is nothing false." "How do you know me?" Nathanael asked. Jesus answered, "I saw you while you were still under the fig tree before Philip called you."

Then Nathanael declared, "Rabbi, you are the Son of God; you are the King of Israel." Jesus said, "You believe because I told you I saw you under the fig tree. You shall see greater things than that." He then added, "I tell you the truth, you shall see heaven open, and the angels of God ascending on the son of Man."

My question is this - What has changed? What is different - today from then?

The story is quite simple. John, the Baptiser, the fire-and-brimstone heart-tugging desert preacher had seen something - the spirit coming down like a dove on a person being baptised. He saw something - the end of his ministry was at hand. John said: *"I came to baptise with water - he who comes after me will baptise with the Holy Spirit."*

All he did was see something apparently no one else saw. He knew his ministry was coming to an end. And so, on the next day, in the middle of teaching two disciples, when he saw this dove stooped man, John stopped, turned, pointed and with convinced thrill, admiration, wonder said *"Behold, the Lamb of God!"*

The title 'Lamb' was laced with layers of meaning. In Israelite thought this was a title for a victim, someone who was gullible enough to be taken advantage of, plotted against, like a gentle lamb led to the slaughter, like Jeremiah not recognizing the plot against him until it is too late (Jeremiah 11:18ff), like the ram caught in a thicket not realizing it was stuck there to take the place of a son named Isaac (Genesis 22:8), like a lamb before its shearers is dumb (Isaiah 53). In today's language we might call him a sucker, one who falls for the plot without defending himself.

Now there were more overtones to the title Lamb because for John and for every faithful Israelite, there was the sacrificial lamb, the lamb that takes away sin, as John had mentioned the day before, *"Behold the Lamb of God who takes away the sin of the world!"*

But on this day, there is no mention of sins, just *"Behold - the Lamb of God."* Trembling words rolling of an orator's coarse tongue. And the two disciples turned and followed him.

All they heard was a title, all they saw was a man and the two disciples turned and followed him. John the baptiser now left alone wiggling his toes in the sand mumbling "the one who comes after me has surpassed me because he was before me ..."

What has changed? What is different - today from then?

They heard the name Lamb, they saw him, they followed. Answers seem to come easy. These two disciples were already disciples! Andrew and John were quick to follow, all too eager to trust the next religious guru. We are more careful today, we have so many more rational tools to make good decisions about the rest of our lives, that's why we're so reluctant to follow! That must be the difference - or is it?

What follows is a cascade. One day of being with this man called the Lamb of God, the one who falls for the ploy, and Andrew goes and finds his brother Simon. Simon is a driven man - not to follow but to fish. Fishing is his career; it's in his character. He has invested in the boat. His hands are calloused and cut from hauling and repairing nets. He knows the places to drop his nets; he gets there before the morning light to catch his haul.

This is no disciple! Simon is a successful businessman with considerable skills and investments as any water faring fisherman among us would well understand. A boat is not called a hole in the water into which you endlessly pour money without a reason. But Simon seems to know when to fish or cut bait - he walks away from his boat, his investments, his skills. He follows.

What has changed? What is different - today from then?

Parents and career counsellors would shake their heads. Bad decision! That young man's future is gone. Is Simon Peter deranged? Why leave all and follow? Such sacrifices at such an early age, think of your future, your career, don't be so stupid Simon...

What has changed? What is different - today from then? Simon was not the only one. Jesus went and found Philip and he said to Philip *"Follow me."*

This time there is no introduction, no title "*the Lamb of God,*" just a command - Follow me! And Philip follows! No resume required. No credentials shown!

And on top of that, Philip does what he will do for the rest of his life so naturally - he runs and tells Nathanael, "*We have found the one Moses wrote about in the Law, and about whom the prophets also wrote - Jesus of Nazereth, the son of Joseph.*"

Upon meeting Jesus, he has already turned into Philip the evangelist, something that he would continue doing throughout the book of Acts till the end of his life.

What has changed? What is different - today from then?

Today to say to our neighbours; "*We have found Jesus!*" - many of us would prefer to voluntarily pull our teeth. We need a degree in theology. We need to grow more in our faith. We'll have more time in an imaginary tomorrow. Our excuses for silence are piled high.

What has changed? What is different - today from then?

How is it that Philip, upon simply hearing the command, turns immediately into a witness? Maybe we are just much more sceptical than these young men were, or are we? Nathanael's first response to Philip's message was, "*Can anything worthwhile come out of the garbage town Nazareth.*"

This is scepticism - but his scepticism is broken by one thing "*Come and see!*" In coming to see, Nathanael discovers that Jesus saw him first, under the fig tree. His life was changed. "*Rabbi, you are the Son of God, you are the King of Israel.*"

What has changed? What is different - today from then?

All of these lives, one after another, turned in a radically different direction and all they did was see Jesus, *"... the Word become flesh, the glory of the One and Only who came from the Father full of grace and truth; the Lamb of God who takes away the sin of the world."* And their lives were changed.

Oh - that must be the difference - they could see Jesus, that was over 2,000 years ago. All they saw was Jesus - the man at the very beginning of his ministry, they turned and followed. Today, we see so much more!

Take the scriptures; see His miracles; His compassion; see the truth through His words, see Jesus turn His face to Jerusalem; intentionally become the Lamb led to the slaughter; hear judge Pontius Pilate proclaim Him innocent; hear those with deceitful schemes call Him guilty; and He willingly falls for the plot; a Lamb before his shearers dumb; watch the whip, then the nails; behold Him raised up, glorified on the cross, cry out *"It is finished!"* the sky is dark; the earth shakes; graves are ripped open - we see him - the Lamb of God, dead, buried, into the third day the silence of the tomb, then the silence is broken, *"He is not here, he has arisen."* Death is conquered; the grave is no longer final.

We see this clearer than the first disciples did. Yet we seem so reluctant to follow, follow radically, expensively, with lives changed in earnest repentance, with evangelistic zeal that everyone notices.

What has changed? What is different - today from then?

Is it that we do <u>not</u> see? And do we not see because we are not looking? Is our reluctance because many of us don't look into the scriptures, don't research diligently to see the Lord of Glory? Are our lives to distracted by keeping our fish nets mended?

Are our eyes turned away to entertainment, to the future, to stocks and bonds, to the bright lights of our culture? Have our accomplishments blinded us to the Light of the world just as city lights blind us to the glory of the stars above? All these first disciples did was Look - they saw Jesus, the Lamb of God, they turned and followed.

What has changed? What is different - today from then?

We know so much more about Jesus than they did back then. Why is it so much harder for us to leave stuff behind and follow Him? Why were they able to commit everything to Him and His people and we are struggling to commit a few hours a week. How is it that we are basking in the glow of God's grace and yet that grace is having very little effect.

We claim to have a real faith and say that we are followers of Jesus and yet we are not in the same place as He is. He is seeking God's children and saving lost souls, and we are seeking our comfort and saving ourselves as much embarrassment and effort as possible.

Have we really seen Jesus? Have we really beheld His glory? Have we been captivated by His majesty such that we are more than happy to let go of the things of this world we hold so dear and follow Him wherever He goes - like those first disciples? They hung off His every word. They couldn't get enough teaching.

Are you like that? Are you thirsty for truth ... hungry for the meat of His word? Perhaps you are. What about all those who are not in church on Sunday ... but still claim to be His followers. Are they hungry for His word?

Do you realise that our online church is now a hundred times greater than our Sunday gathering?

I see the same hunger in many of them that I see in those early disciples and I get more feedback, questions and interaction from my teaching from people I have never met around the world ... every week ... than I do from people who receive that teaching face-to-face.

I know that there are people here who connect with all kinds of teaching during the week and they don't need to connect with what comes from this church in order to be fed. And yet I believe there is something very special and very important about what is preached in a local church context. Whether the preacher is good or bad is irrelevant ... God honours the local church and speaks a very specific word to that church first.

You may be connecting to God's word to others all around the world ... but are you connecting to God's word to your local church – is it a priority for you? Do you really believe that it is God Who arranges the parts of the body and they whatever pastor or teacher you have at this point in your journey is someone God led to you and has given him a message for you and your fellow worshippers?

I believe we have missed something very important in our understanding of the place and importance and integrity of the local church. So back to annoying, repetitive question:

What has changed? What is different - today from then?

Do you see the same passion and commitment and total surrender to Jesus today as you see when you read of those first disciples? Do you see it in yourself or in those around you? If the answer is no, then why is that so? Could it be that we have not really seen Jesus - not the way they saw Him? That is a confronting question, especially to those of us who have called ourselves His disciple for many years.

Has your heart been captured by the holy calling of the Lord? Have you been arrested by His charisma and His heart and His passion for the lost children of God? Are you still tending your nets and looking after your worldly interests, as you look at Jesus from a distance, where it's safe?

Or have you dropped the nets and anything else in your hands and your heart that stands in the way of your commitment to the Lord of Glory and declared are you ready to follow Him, wherever He goes, and do whatever He calls you to do?

Let me ask you one final question, in light of what the Spirit of God has shown you in this sermon, how then shall you live? In other words, what choices will you make tomorrow in light of what God has shown you today? If you truly want to seize the day, you must answer this question.

6. BLOOM WHERE YOU'RE PLANTED

How would you characterise your level of contentment? When you look at your life, how would you describe the feelings you have toward it? Look at the various component parts of your life. So many things are involved - where you work; where you live; who you're married to or not; how much money you have, how much education you have; how much you weigh; your current health; how many opportunities you have; and so on.

We could go through each item and you could rate your level of satisfaction or dissatisfaction on each one. Let's say 1 = total dissatisfaction and 10 = incomparable metaphysical bliss. After rating each item you could then calculate the average of all your scores and then discover your overall level of satisfaction with your lot in life.

Where do you think you would be? Would you be singing the little chorus that goes, "*I'm so happy, so very happy, I've got the love of Jesus in my heart,*" or would you be singing with the Rolling Stones, "*I can't get no satisfaction*"?

When you think about it, there probably is a lot in every one of our lives that we would like to change. All of us could have some level of dissatisfaction about many things. But the two questions I would like to ask are these: Where does that come from and where does it lead?

Where do you think your dissatisfaction comes from? In other words, why are you dissatisfied? You might think that is a stupid question. You are dissatisfied because you're not happy with the situation. But it might not be as simple as that. You see, you are assuming that your unhappiness is a healthy response to a bad situation.

Have you ever considered that you may be unhappy because your perspective has been altered? It may be that you have been programmed to be unhappy.

Our whole society promotes dissatisfaction with life. In some ways, it is built into the foundation of our economic system of capitalism. Goods and services are marketed through advertising, and the goal of advertising is to create a felt need for the product.

They want to convince you that you need this new thing. What you have is not good enough. If you could only get the new, the improved, the bigger and better whatever, the quality of your life would take a giant step forward … and we fall for it.

Sadly, sometimes it is applied to more than a better brand of toothpaste. Often people think that if they could only get that new husband or wife, they would be better off. And they fall for it. This consumerist approach to life comes at us from every direction. The incessant bombardment we receive through advertisements on TV, radio, billboards, the internet, and in magazines and newspapers, re-programs our minds to think a certain way about things, and about what brings real happiness.

The message is that if only our situation were different, we would be happier and more fulfilled. The situation is what is at fault. It's that sorry old job. If only I had a different one. It's those extra 10 kilos. If only I could be a little thinner.

You fill in the blank. If only I could change _____ , I will be happy. And where does all this lead? Well, it leads in many directions, none of them positive. It leads to a general dissatisfaction with life, as well as further unhappiness.

Perhaps worst of all, it keeps you from being the man or woman of God that you were created to be because it leads you to believe that you are not in a position to serve God fully. It stops you from seizing the day and making the most of the opportunities God has given you.

If only you could change this or that, then you could really serve God. But not now. Not in your current situation. This is the lie that Paul will address in our text today. And it is something you need to address in your life as well or you will be held in miserable bondage to it for the rest of your unhappy life.

> **1 Corinthians 7:17-20** *"Nevertheless, each person should live as a believer in whatever situation the Lord has assigned to them, just as God has called them. This is the rule I lay down in all the churches. Was a man already circumcised when he was called? He should not become uncircumcised. Was a man uncircumcised when he was called? He should not be circumcised. Circumcision is nothing and uncircumcision is nothing. Keeping God's commands is what counts. Each person should remain in the situation they were in when God called them."*

God wants you to bloom where you have been planted. He can use you right now, in the situation in which you find yourself. Unless it is a sinful situation that you need to abandon, He can show you His purpose for using that situation for your good and for His glory.

So, if you want to learn the secret of godly contentment and true peace, look at our text today. In Paul's message to these confused Corinthian Christians, we will see clearly what we are to focus on.

Don't focus on secondary situations!

One of the most important lessons of our text is this: Don't focus on secondary situations. What are these secondary situations? Paul makes it quite clear that they are the circumstances of life in which we find ourselves. They are our job situation, our financial situation, our marriage and family situation, our health situation and the like. This is quite clear from the context. He has been discussing marriage and instructing them to stay together. He now expands that thought to other areas of our lives.

> *"Was a man already circumcised when he was called? He should not become uncircumcised. Was a man uncircumcised when he was called? He should not be circumcised. <u>Circumcision is nothing</u> and uncircumcision is nothing. (7:18-19a) Were you a slave when you were called? <u>Don't let it trouble you</u> - although if you can gain your freedom, do so. For he who was a slave when he was called by the Lord is the Lord's freedman; similarly, he who was a free man when he was called is Christ's slave. You were bought at a price; do not become slaves of men." (7:21-23)*

He gives two illustrations of contemporary situations some of these believers would have found themselves in - circumcision and slavery. Can someone who was not circumcised according to the Jewish law really be a true servant of Jesus Christ? Some thought that all male Christians needed to be circumcised.

But here Paul plainly says that neither circumcision nor uncircumcision is important. In fact, he calls it <u>nothing</u>. Pretty strong words to use with a primarily Jewish audience.

Similarly, he doesn't regard slavery as an impediment to serving God. He is not advocating slavery, as some have mistakenly claimed.

He tells them that if they can gain their freedom, they should do so. It is clear that Paul saw the value of being free, but in so far as one's relationship to God was concerned, slavery was not a barrier. One could serve God as a slave just as faithfully as someone who was free. After all, we are all slaves to God. And so Paul tells them - don't let it trouble you.

The message is clear. Our situation in life is secondary. It should not be our primary focus. It certainly should never be an excuse for not serving God. And yet, so many people make it an excuse. If only I didn't have this situation in my life, then I could really serve God. If only I had more money. If only I had a different job. If only my health were better. If only I had a more supportive spouse. If only, if only, if only ... your problem is that you're focusing on the wrong thing.

None of these circumstances should keep you from fully following Jesus Christ. The only situations that have the power to do that are situations where you are living in unrepentant sin. If your lifestyle is against God, then you have a problem.

The fact that you may not have ideal circumstances should never be a problem. It can only be a problem when you allow it to be and that is a problem of your focus. You are focusing on the wrong things. You are allowing secondary situations to become your primary focus.

When you allow these secondary situations to become your primary focus, you become an unhappy and dissatisfied person. You fix your gaze on all the things that you would like to change. You concentrate on what's wrong with your life and the world around you. You mull over and over in your mind the way things 'ought' to be.

You hold a magnifying glass over every little imperfection like a teenager looking at a pimple in a mirror. And pretty soon you have a long list of issues which prove how bad your life is and you're angry at God for doing it all to you. Congratulations. You have just turned into a negative person and you are right where the devil wants you to be. So, what can we do about it? there a way we can avoid this downward spiral of negativity and dissatisfaction? Glad you asked.

Keep the main thing the main thing!

It's not good enough to simply say that we need to avoid focusing on secondary situations. Have you ever tried to not think of something? The harder you try to not think of it, the more you are unable to think of anything else. Our minds abhor a vacuum. Rather, we need to positively focus on something else.

Simply put, we need to keep the main thing the main thing. We need to aim our focus at the primary reason for living as a Christian. And what does Paul say that is? Keeping God's commands is what counts. (7:19)

Here we have spelled out for us the central focus of a life which is lived for God. It is to keep God's commandments. It is to be pleasing to God by living according to his will for us. That is what really counts. That is the main thing for the Christian. Our challenge is to keep it the main thing. Instead of focusing on all the other situations that are not ideal, we need to focus on living a life fully committed to following Jesus Christ.

No life is ideal. The richest people in the world probably still complain over a wide host of problems they face.

Christina Onassis, who had a tax-free income of over one million dollars a week, and who tragically died at age 37 of what many believe was the result of a life of drug abuse, once commented, "Happiness is not based on money and the greatest proof of that is our family!"

All of us are challenged in one way or another. No life is perfect and some of us experience serious difficulties from time to time. The measure of a person is not the absence of adversity. It is how he or she responds to adversity. And the only way we will respond properly is to have the proper perspective of our lives.

Having a better situation will not necessarily mean that our lives will count for anything. It will not necessarily mean we will be any happier or more satisfied. The greatest things in life are actually not things at all.

Make Jesus the centre of your life. I'm not talking about giving lip service here. I'm not talking about having a warm feeling in your heart for the Lord. I'm talking about actually living for him. I'm talking about abandoning our excuses, taking stock of how we are living, and changing whatever needs to be changed in our lives that is not consistent with God's will. I'm talking about making sure God and His will are the main thing.

Does God really count in your life? How do you know? You know by whether you are willing to do what He wants. When you and I really begin to live out what we say we believe, then and only then do we begin to experience the peace and contentment that we desperately need and desire. For the first time in a long time, we can truly relax. We can breathe a sigh of relief in the knowledge that it all doesn't depend on what we can bring to the table.

God is not impressed by what we have and His work in our lives is not hindered by what we don't have. In fact, we may very well be in the exact situation that God wants us in.

Remember - God Called You

Sometimes we forget that God is sovereign. Remember that God called you. And when He called you, He knew everything about you - not just about your past, but also about your future. He knew all about the circumstances of your life. And He not only called you, but He desires for you to serve Him in the midst of your unique circumstances.

"Nevertheless, each one should retain the place in life that the Lord assigned to him and to which God has called him. This is the rule I lay down in all the churches." (7:17) "Each one should remain in the situation which he was in when God called him." (7:20) "Brothers, each man, as responsible to God, should remain in the situation God called him to." (7:24)

It is clear from these passages that God has a plan for your life that includes using the situations of your life for his glory. You don't need to change those situations in order to be used of God. You just need to ask yourself how you can be obedient in the midst of those circumstances. Remember that God called you and that He knows what He's doing. And you also need to remember that God has the power to change anything in your life He desires to change. Until He does, why not trust him?

God is calling us to bloom where we are planted. God is aware of our situation. Our challenge is to be God's man or God's woman, living as a Christian ought to live, and responding as a Christian ought to respond, as we deal with what has been dealt to us.

Two things will happen. The first is that our own feeling about life will change. We will begin to see how many gifts we have been given and how much we have for which to be thankful. The mountains will become molehills once again and we will simply step over them or walk around them. Our level of peace will increase and pessimism will be replaced by optimism and hope. In short, God will do something in our hearts. We will become better people - people of joy.

The second thing that will happen is that others will notice the difference. They will see the difference that God makes in a person who is committed to living their lives by the principles of His word.

As we face the common difficulties of the majority of people on planet Earth, people will come to understand that following Jesus is not pie in the sky in the sweet by and by, but a practical faith that deals with life as it is. In short, we will be a living testimony of the power of the grace of God when we bloom where we are planted. Then, we will be able to truly seize the day.

7. BREAKING OUT OF A RUT

Have you ever been stuck in a rut? There are many ruts in life. If you've done no exercise for many years, you'll probably find you are in a fitness rut that resists change. There are other ruts in life as well. Getting started on a new project can be difficult when you are stuck in the rut of procrastination. Some ruts are good, I suppose. Habitual behaviour is a great thing if it is the right habit that captivates you. But more often than not, when we say we are stuck in a rut, we mean that we are having difficulty escaping a wrong behaviour.

Someone has said, "*A rut is nothing but a grave with the ends kicked out.*" Another said, "*Many have the right aim in life - they just never get around to pulling the trigger.*" Probably all of us get the wheels of our lives stuck in ruts from time to time, so in this sermon I'd like us to look at a story in the Bible of a man who was in about the deepest rut anyone could ever experience. Most people of his day considered his rut to be inescapable. His name was Bartimaeus and he was a blind beggar who lived in the ancient city of Jericho. Let's pick up on Mark's account in his gospel.

> **Mark 10:46-52** *"Then they came to Jericho. As Jesus and his disciples, together with a large crowd, were leaving the city, a blind man, Bartimaeus (which means "son of Timaeus"), was sitting by the roadside begging. When he heard that it was Jesus of Nazareth, he began to shout, "Jesus, Son of David, have mercy on me!" Many rebuked him and told him to be quiet, but he shouted all the more, "Son of David, have mercy on me!"*
>
> *Jesus stopped and said, "Call him." So they called to the blind man, "Cheer up! On your feet! He's calling you."*

Throwing his cloak aside, he jumped to his feet and came to Jesus. "What do you want me to do for you?" Jesus asked him. The blind man said, "Rabbi, I want to see."

"Go," said Jesus, "your faith has healed you." Immediately he received his sight and followed Jesus along the road."

Let me take a moment to sketch out for you, the kind of rut poor old Bart found himself in. First, he was blind. In his day, a blind man couldn't work. He couldn't read or write. 15-year-old Louis Braille would not invent a revolutionary communication method for at least another 1,800 years! He couldn't even get around. I know there were no 'seeing eye dogs' in that day because dogs were unclean animals to the Jews and they were not used as companions for the blind until 1916. So poor old Bart was reduced to begging.

A man in his condition, unless he had relatives to support him, could do little else but sit near a popular thoroughfare and cry out, "*Alms, Alms for the poor!*" He was also an object of pity. I say that because that was the key to him making a living. It was only by soliciting the sympathy of others that he could survive, and he probably got pretty good at what he did.

Finally, for the most part, his life was reduced to those last four words of verse 46: "*sitting by the road.*" That was his rut. Blind. Begging. Pitied. Sitting by the road. For most people, such obstacles would be considered inescapable. But Bartimaeus got out of his rut. The purpose of this sermon is to show you how he did it and how you can get out of any rut you find yourself in as well.

There are several things Bartimaeus did that day when Jesus passed by his begging station that helped get him out of his rut.

Yes, I know it could be said that it was Jesus Who made him well - something he could not do for himself. Nonetheless, had Bartimaeus not done these things and gotten out of his very deep rut, he would never have been healed. The actions Bartimaeus took that day suggest several things you and I can do when we find our lives so confined that it could be said we are in a rut.

As I progress through this chapter, I will phrase each principle as though I were pointing the Biblical principle right at you personally. I hope you will take it that way, realising, of course, that it applies to all of us. The first, and most important principle is this:

1. *Assume responsibility for your own life ...*

Verse 47 says, *"When he heard that it was Jesus of Nazareth, he began to shout, 'Jesus, Son of David, have mercy on me!'"* Notice here that Bartimaeus took the initiative himself to cry out. That is a very important observation, perhaps the most important of the seven initiatives he took that day.

Do you remember the days of your childhood when, if you were uncomfortable, or afraid, or hurting, you could always count on mum or dad or maybe some relative to take care of you? *"You don't have to be afraid,"* you were reassured. *"I'll take care of you."* Then, for most of you, you left your home, an action that was perhaps, at first, a little scary. Could you make it on your own? Would you have to run back to mum and dad in humiliation?

You probably did a lot of growing up in those first couple of years on your own. Perhaps the best definition there is to describe someone who is truly 'grown up' is one who has assumed responsibility for his or her own life.

One reason a rut is so hard to break out of is that it is secure. It is safe. It's comfortable. Like those easy days when you could count on mum and dad. Oh, we make all kinds of excuses, but really, there is very little risk in doing the same thing that has always carried you through in the past. From the bottom of our ruts we ask, *"Why should I give up what is comfortable in exchange for something untried?"*

Someone as handicapped as Bartimaeus could certainly be subject to such reasoning. He probably wouldn't have to look too far to find those who would support him in his thinking. No, he didn't particularly enjoy sitting there beside the road, but at least it was comfortable. It's what he knew. It's what he did well. Being dependent upon others wasn't the most rewarding lifestyle, but at least he knew what he would be doing tomorrow and the next day. Yet he dreamed of more. He dreamed of being able to see.

That day when Jesus passed by, Bartimaeus was suddenly faced with the biggest decision of his life. Would he continue to be dependent upon others where he felt safe, or would he assume responsibility for himself and risk climbing out of his rut? For every Bartimaeus in this world who risks getting out of a rut, there are probably a thousand who shrink back, unwilling to take that risk.

Think for a moment about whatever rut you may be in. Yes, you can continue to blame your parents or the society or your nationality or your rotten luck in life or your lack of self-discipline or the 'fat' genes you inherited from your parents or the weather or the government or whatever. You certainly have the freedom to do that. But there is a price to pay for that dubious 'freedom.' You'll be a rut dweller the rest of your life. You might as well quit dreaming. Don't bother hoping. Quit thinking about the day when your ship will come in or someone will reach down and pull you out.

Unless you take responsibility for your life and your situation, nothing will change. Then comes the next really important thing that anyone stuck in a rut needs to do.

2. *Believe you can change ...*

For Bartimaeus, it took some real faith that day to cast aside his cloak, jump up, and move in the direction of the sound of the crowd surrounding Jesus. That faith comes from a deep belief that things can change. Verse 52 says, "*Go your way; your faith has made you well.*"

Where does that belief and faith come from, anyway? Are we talking about a kind of hopeful leap in the dark when we talk of believing you can change? I don't think so. Faith must be based upon some evidence, otherwise it is nothing more than gullibility.

Notice that phrase in verse 47, "*And when he heard that it was Jesus the Nazarene, he began to cry out ...*" That implies some recognition - some prior knowledge. Bartimaeus had probably heard on the grapevine that Jesus was a healer. There are descriptions of at least six people who were healed of blindness in the New Testament. There were probably many more. Bart would have heard of at least some of these.

How does that apply to you and me? The Bible says, in Romans 10:17, "*So faith comes from hearing, and hearing by the word of Christ.*" Hearing such stories produces faith! And that is one of the great blessings of the Bible. It is full of stories of people who, with God's help, overcame tremendous odds and escaped deep ruts. Besides that, there are many reassuring principles to cheer us on. Not only that, but there are also contemporary stories that can be told as well.

That is one reason we gather to look into God's Word and encourage one another and share our testimonies every Sunday. You don't get that outside these walls very often. Out there most people don't believe you can change. They're busy perfecting the art of blaming others and explaining why change is impossible. They've made so many excuses for themselves and others that anything beyond mediocrity now sounds impossible.

There is sufficient evidence both in the Bible and in experience to assure you that you can break out of your rut. But you must avail yourself to it by believing you can change.

3. Clarify what you really need ...

Notice in verse 51 what Jesus asked Bartimaeus: *"What do you want Me to do for you?"* Why did Jesus ask that? Couldn't He just read the man's mind? Didn't He already know? You see, the question wasn't asked for Jesus' benefit. It was asked for Bartimaeus' benefit and those who watched on.

Seldom do any of us do anything about the ruts we live in until our circumstances force us to. Even then, we seldom move until we get to the place where we set a goal. I suspect some of you have given up setting any goals in your life. You've said something to this effect: *"I've failed to hit my targets before, so I'll just quit making commitments. That way it won't be obvious if I fail."*

But a life with no goals is the life of a rut-dweller. If you have no goals - you quit dreaming, forget hope and your chance of hitting something you don't aim at is virtually nil. Certainly if you hope to break out of a rut, you have to be willing to clarify what it is you really need and want!"

What do you want Me to do for you?" Jesus asked. Bartimaeus didn't hesitate: *"Rabbi, I want to see!"*

4. Stop worrying about what other people will say ...

Something that keeps many of us trapped in our ruts is the fear of disapproval from others. Think of a guy who wants to get started on an exercise program. He figures his best bet is to get into the local exercise gym with a one-year membership. So he calls, signs up, and sends in the money. But he never goes. Why? Well, let me tell you what often happens - and when you've heard this, you'll understand why those who own such businesses want their money in advance!

He probably went down and bought the flashy singlet and the shorts with the stripe up the side. He probably got the set of shoes they recommended, paying more for them than he ever paid for shoes. Then the big day came. He got into the car and drove to the gym. If he was brave, he got out and went in. As he walked through the door and looked around, what did he see? He saw ten or twenty trim, hard bodies twenty years his junior, working out. That's what he saw.

Then, as he looked down at his middle-aged belly hanging over his pants and considered what he would look like and what might be said under the breaths of every person in the gym that looked at him, he turned and walked out and never came back, even if it meant he'd lose a full year of fees. It's a common story, told every year all across the country.

Bartimaeus didn't have to imagine what others would say if he stepped forward that day. They told him.

Verse 48 says, "*And many were sternly telling him to be quiet, but he kept crying out all the more, "Son of David, have mercy on me!"* You see, he had to push past what other people said.

What you and I have to realize is that the vast majority of people making up the human race are critics. They're pessimists. Not only that, but they are also fickle. You see, since most people who attempt to climb out of a rut end up climbing back in, people around get to believing that is the norm.

That is what is expected. Most of them aren't willing to risk encouraging someone who won't be daunted by those odds. They might get laughed at for making such rash predictions! So they take the safe route. They conclude you won't make it. They opt for what they figure will be the winning side. And so they discourage you.

That's why the Bible warns us about the company we keep. If we hang around and listen to fearful or negative people, we'll become fearful or negative. I find it interesting that in certain key battles in the Old Testament, God sent those who were fearful home, even though it lessened the number of troops. Now I also said they are fickle.

That is best illustrated in our text. Verse 48 as we've already seen, says *"Many rebuked him and told him to be quiet."* You can almost hear them now, can't you? *"Shut up, Bartimaeus! The Rabbi isn't interested in people like you! Besides, what could he do for you? People like you are better off quiet."* Did he listen? No he didn't!

Then look what happened. Verse 49 says, *"And Jesus stopped and said, 'Call him.'" And they called the blind man, saying to him, "Cheer up! On your feet! He's calling you."* Talk about fickle!

In one breath they are saying, *"Shut up, Bartimaeus!"* Then, when they saw Jesus was willing to respond, they quickly jumped on the other side of the fence!

Do you see why you must stop worrying about what other people will say? What they say so often is totally irrelevant to you. They're only saying what they figure is the safest thing to say. If you make it out of your rut, they'll say they knew all along you could do it!

Now I'm not saying we should never get good counsel from godly people. But if you listen to the crowd; you'll stay in your rut! Guaranteed! Stop worrying about what other people will say!

5. *Stop waiting for ideal circumstances ...*

The situation on the day Bartimaeus was healed was far from ideal. Verse 46 says that Jesus was going out from Jericho with His disciples and a great multitude. What chance did anyone have of getting Jesus' attention in such a crowd? Hardly any. So what chance did a blind man have?

Perhaps Bartimaeus should have waited for a better time. Maybe tomorrow or the next day or next week or next year. Maybe he'd be braver on his birthday or on New Year's Day. That's classic rut dweller language, isn't it? Waiting for ideal circumstances will leave you in a rut - a rut that could ultimately become a grave. Stop waiting for those ideal circumstances.

6. *Do something bold and dramatic ...*

We're talking about risk here aren't we? It's scary! Probably some of you have already dismissed all this and decided to keep to the security of your rut.

That's certainly you're choice. But at least be honest about it. Quit blaming others. Bartimaeus put it all out front for everyone to see. Verse 50 says, *"Throwing his cloak aside, he jumped to his feet and came to Jesus."* What a big, bold, open, public stand to take! He was determined to get out of his rut!

A young man once sought out an older, successful executive for some advice. He found him at his beach front home. After introducing himself, he asked if the older man would counsel him on the ins and outs of being successful in business. At that request, the older man asked the younger one to accompany him down to the beach.

As they were walking along, suddenly the older man grabbed the younger and dragged him out into the surf. In one swift movement, he thrust the man's head under the water and held him down. In panic, the younger man fought the older man's grasp.

When he was about to black out, the older man loosened his grip and let him up. After regaining his breath, the younger man asked what on earth was going on. He never forgot the man's reply – he said, "*When you want success as badly as you wanted that air, you'll most probably get it.*"

That's really the issue, isn't it? Too often we think we want to get out of our rut, but we really don't - at least we don't want it badly enough to do whatever it takes to be free from what entraps us. Are you willing to do something bold? Are you willing to take a stand in front of others? "*I don't think something that drastic is necessary,*" you might say. Maybe not, but have your less drastic measures worked for you? Maybe it's time to get bold! Do something bold and dramatic. Finally, if you want to break out of a rut ...

7. *Make your move now!*

Perhaps nothing keeps people in ruts longer than procrastination. Bartimaeus had no idea Jesus was coming to his town that day. The day was just like every other day to him as he climbed off his sleeping pallet and felt his way down to his familiar spot beside the road. He didn't have time to prepare. It was suddenly just there. I am not suggesting that you shouldn't take time to plan. But do something now or this occasion will pass by and become just like all the others where you didn't break out of your rut. Make your move now!

I hope you'll consider using these seven principles when you find yourself in a rut. Let me say one more thing before I finish. Perhaps the most dangerous rut a person can be in is one that leads them away from God. With that in mind, let me close with this haunting poem.

'Those Wasted Years'
by Theodore W. Brennan

I looked upon a farm one day, that once I used to own
The barn had fallen to the ground, the fields were overgrown
The house in which my children grew, where we had lived for years
I turned to see it broken down and brushed aside the tears.

I looked upon my soul one day, to find it too had grown
With thorns and nettles everywhere, the seeds neglect had sown
The years had passed while I had cared for things of lesser worth
The things of heaven I let go, when minding things of earth

To Christ I turned with bitter tears and cried, "O Lord, forgive!
I haven't much time left for You, not many years to live."
The wasted years forever gone, the days I can't recall
If I could live those days again, I'd make Him Lord of all.

The Bible says, "*Today is the day of salvation.*" If you are stuck in a rut that is leading you away from God, today is the day to get out! Do it now!

If you don't, you will never seize the day.

8. FOR SUCH A TIME AS THIS

From my observation over the past twenty years, I am firmly convinced that God is waking the 'sleeping giant.' He is shaking the church from its slumber and calling His people to stand up and be counted. However, God is doing this in a way that most Christians are not used to and most churches have not been prepared for.

God is not, in my opinion, calling Christians to march in the streets with Bibles in hand or book football stadiums for evangelistic rallies. That is not the season I see emerging for the church in this nation. God is mobilising His army in a different way. He is calling them to interact with people around them on their own turf; in their own language and in a way that they can relate to.

In other words, God is calling us to manifest or 'incarnate' the life of Christ in the most practical possible ways in the communities and sub-communities in which we find ourselves: schools, universities, TAFE, workplaces, shops, governments, social and service clubs, sporting clubs, our neighbourhood ... etc.

Why is God moving this way? Well, first of all, God is moving us into this 'marketplace' ministry more and more because that is where we should have always been in the first place. Whether you call this 'lifestyle evangelism' ... 'relationship evangelism' or 'incarnational ministry' ... this not new at all. In fact, Jesus was the One Who first introduced it. He did it, He showed us how to do it and then He left us to do it on His behalf.

The second reason why God is moving in this direction is because the institutionalised church has lost its influence in society.

The church, as an organisation; and as an institution; has increasingly over the past 20 years, become marginalised and is now largely irrelevant in our nation. That can change. That will change … but not in the way many people think.

The church in this nation will not grow and become more effective by just running better 'church' programs and activities within the confines of the church structure and buildings. If that worked, we would have full buildings right across the nation because the institutionalised church has never run so many programs and events.

God is energising and mobilising people 'on the job' … 'on the front-line' of the battle … which is in the places where unchurched people gather and are relaxed and comfortable. At work, at the footy games, in schools, at the doctors' waiting room, supermarkets, bank queues etc. I am always excited when I hear the stories of people's conversations in these places and how God has gone before them and opened doors for them to speak about their faith.

In that interaction with people 'out there' we soon discover a very real need and a very serious concern which Christians across our nation must take to heart. This is not new by any means, this need has existed for a long time, but our awareness of it must increase as I believe this issue, in general terms at least, will be the primary catalyst for the advance of the Kingdom of God in the coming days.

Our Christian heritage as a nation is being forgotten and we are headed for very choppy waters if the current trend is not reversed. Like sheep without a shepherd and a ship without a rudder, this great nation is heading for peril if the people of God do not wake up, start praying … and talking … and voting … and re-establishing that solid foundation.

If a nation forgets its Christian heritage and history and is ignorant of the Biblical principles upon which it was built, that nation is in danger of losing its freedom. We must teach the younger generation their Christian heritage and not leave it to teachers to omit such information because of their religious beliefs (or lack of them)!

We must stand up for our heritage and freedom or risk losing it! It is frightening to see what can happen to a nation that forgets its Christian heritage. Nazi Germany is one horrendous example. If you were to visit the Nazi death camps in Germany and inspect the gas chambers where thousands were murdered, you would see photographic records of the pitiful faces gazing down at you, including many Christians. You would also see a plaque which reads: *"Those who forget their history are bound to repeat the same mistakes"*.

After the first world war, Germany virtually became a fatherless nation, almost an entire generation of males had perished in the war. Without fathers in that culture, there was no one to teach the German children their heritage thus creating a perfect climate for the rise of Hitler. He was able to use his knowledge of German heritage and history to enslave its young people through the Hitler Youth Movement, and eventually the whole nation. Hitler said: "A *man who has no sense of history, is a man who has no ears or eyes."*

Communist leader Karl Marx once said: "*A people without a heritage are easily persuaded."* The communist dictum was "*Capture the youth and you capture the nation."* It happened in Germany and Russia through war. It's happening in Australia, but this time through moral abandonment and a complete loss of identity as a nation – while the church seems powerless, as it watches this decay.

Contrary to what has been taught in many circles over the years, Australia has a wonderful Christian heritage, a heritage of which we can be proud! Let me just say that when I speak of our Christian heritage, I am not speaking only about an Anglo-Saxon heritage. It doesn't matter what colour, class, or race - there is neither Jew nor Greek. I am talking about our Australian Christian heritage!

From reading the Scriptures, it would seem that birthright (the passing of the Father's blessing) is very important to God. The first-born son inherited a double portion as well as the blessing of the father.

In Genesis 25:29-34 we see where Esau sold his birthright, inheritance or heritage to his younger brother Jacob for nothing more than some stew. From then on, the blessings ceased to flow to Esau and flowed to Jacob. It was he who handed those blessings or the heritage on to Joseph. Few people look at Biblical faith as a heritage, but God does! He says: "*I am the God of Abraham, and of Isaac, and of Jacob.*" He speaks in terms of generations. He speaks of fathers who pass on their spiritual heritage from one generation to another. Why? Because He is establishing a heritage of faith.

Many Australians place little value on their Christian heritage, often 'selling it' for short term gain. These are critical days for our nation. There are moves afoot to strip this "*South Land of the Holy Spirit*" of its Christian heritage. Some may even be tempted to doubt that anti-Christian humanistic forces could grow so powerful in Australia, even in a republican Australia.

But consider what Manning Clark is quoted as saying about the late Lionel Murphy: *'It had been one of Murphy's aims to dismantle the Judeo-Christian ethic of Australian society.'* (Page 8, Sydney Morning Herald, 30.10.86).

Murphy's protégé, Gareth Evans, a former president of the humanist society, and architect of the proposed *'Bill of Rights,'* was himself quoted as saying: "children want a light to sexual freedom and education and 'protection from the influence of Christianity." (Page 8, SMH 7/5/76).

> **Psalm 78:1-8** *"O my people, listen to my teaching ... I will teach you hidden lessons from our past   stories our ancestors handed down to us. We will not hide these truths from our children but will tell the next generation about the glorious deeds of the Lord. We will tell of his power and the mighty miracles he did ... He commanded our ancestors to teach them to their children, so the next generation might know them   even the children not yet born so they in turn might teach them to their children. So each generation can set its hope anew on God, remembering his glorious miracles and obeying his commands."*

The key point here for parents is to teach the children their heritage, while the key word to the children is "remember." Why do we need to remind them? "That they may set their hope in God. And not forget the works of God."

In the story of Esther we find the exact opposite of Esau's dilemma. It is the story of a Jewish girl who was raised by a relative, one of the nation's leading men by the name of Mordecai. Esther, the beautiful Jewess, soon caught the eye of the king and he married her, but Esther concealed her Jewish heritage. (Esther 2:16-20). The king's main leader, Haman, was an unscrupulous man who tricked the king into signing a decree that all the Jews were to be killed.

Mordecai then came to Esther imploring her to go before the king and plead for the lives of her people the Jews. However to come before the king if not summoned could mean death. Mordecai speaks these prophetic words to her:

> **Esther 4:13-14** *"... Do not think in your heart that you will escape in the king's palace any more than all the other Jews. For if you remain completely silent at this time, relief and deliverance will arise for the Jews from another place, but you and your father's house will perish. Yet who knows whether you have come into the kingdom for such a time as this?"*

Esther could remain silent and live comfortably for the rest of her life. The king did not know that she was a Jew with a death sentence hanging over her head. This was her reply to the king:

> **Esther 7:3:** *"Then Queen Esther answered and said, 'If I have found favour in your sight, O king, and if it pleases the king, let my life be given me at my petition, and my people at my request. For we have been sold, my people and I, to be destroyed, to be killed and to be annihilated ..."*

Her answer continues in verse 6: *"For how can I endure to see the evil that will come upon my people? Or how can I endure to see the destruction of my countrymen?"* The king was infuriated. Who would dare to do such a thing? He asked Esther who it was and she named Haman. The story ends this way: Haman the plotter was hung upon the very gallows he had prepared for Mordecai. Mordecai was promoted to replace Haman, while the Jews received *"light and gladness, joy and honour."* (Esther 8:17).

The Jews were so blessed that many of the people converted to Judaism while Esther was held in honour by the people and loved by the king. Look again at Mordecai's words to her in Esther 4:14: *"Yet who knows whether you have come into the kingdom for such a time as this?"* Esther was placed by God in a strategic place for such a time.

I am astounded at how little Australians know about their Christian heritage. No wonder Australian youth have such horrendous drug and suicide statistics. Many of our youth leave these shores to seek a more 'exciting' life overseas. Hundreds waste their lives on drugs, sex and crime, or bludge on the beach. The strength of our youth is being lost. But we can change it!

Winston Churchill is a classic example of old adage: "*the hand that rocks the cradle rules the world.*" It was neither his mother nor his father who formed Churchill's character and influenced his beliefs, but his Godly nanny Elizabeth Anne Everest. It was she who taught him to pray and memorize scripture. She also taught him his Godly British heritage.

Churchill was so inspired by his heritage that he wrote a six-volume biography about his ancestry. His studies helped shape his entire life and ultimately affected the whole world through his leadership during the dark and terrible days of World War II.

One of the signs of a great society is the diligence with which it passes culture from one generation to the next. This culture is the embodiment of everything the people of that society hold dear: its religious faith, its heroes. When one generation no longer esteems its own heritage and fails to pass the torch to its children, it is saying in essence that the very foundational principles and experiences that make the society what it is are no longer valid.

This leaves that generation without any sense of definition or direction, making them the fulfilment of Karl Marx's dictum, '*A people without a heritage are easily persuaded.*' What is required when this happens and the society has lost its way - is for leaders to arise who have not forgotten the discarded legacy and who love it with all their hearts.

They must become the voice of that lost generation, wooing them back to the faith of the fathers, back to the ancient foundations and the bedrock values.

Winston Churchill was the voice and embodiment of such a heritage. As an historian, Churchill studied societies that disconnected themselves from their historical moorings. He discovered that when a generation isolates itself from its past and begins to measure progress only in terms of its own accumulations, the history of that civilization begins drawing to a close. Churchill concluded that what holds society together from generation to generation are those shared values and traditions that comprise heritage. Civilizations can only thrive from age to age when the legacy each generation receives from its ancestors is passed on in strengthened form to their children.

Through the course of his long life, Churchill had watched the gradual erosion of vital Christianity as a cultural force in England. He grieved at the loss of honour, respect and humility that resulted. Listen to Churchill's warning: *"Those who seek to plan the future should not forget the inheritance they have received from the past. If the present tries to sit in judgment on the past, it will lose the future."*

In 1954, Churchill said this to the Reverent Billy Graham, *"I do not see much hope for the future unless it is the hope you are talking about, young man. We must return to God."* Churchill hoped that the next generation would recover what it had not accepted from the generation before it: faith in God and the culture that faith produces.

Proverbs 22:28 says: *"Do not remove the ancient landmark. Which your fathers have set."* In other words we are to respect and honour the foundations that the nation's founding fathers, have laid down.

Yet some Australians remain blissfully ignorant of their country's Christian heritage and foundations and are continually pushing to change them. Either they have forgotten their nation's history, or in many cases, they have never been taught it in the first place. This has brought disastrous consequences.

In the 1911 national census 95.9% of Australians said they embraced the Christian Faith. In the 1991 census 73.8% of the population confirmed their acceptance of Christianity, while in the 1996 census 70.9% acknowledged their Christian belief. Can you guess what that figure was in the 2021 census? In our most recent census, less than 44% of Australians identified themselves as Christian.

Dr. Graham McLennan, an Australian Christian historian, and my former dentist and co-labourer in the gospel at Orange, once wrote these words: "Obviously we are not yet a nation of Christians. But we should steadfastly resist all who presume upon our Christian tolerance by trying to subvert or deny our Christian heritage. The tolerance, freedom, tranquillity, justice and prosperity we enjoy exists only in that tiny handful of nations that enjoy Biblical Christianity but will diminish quickly if we neglect or depart from that Christian heritage."

Brothers and sisters, I want you to hear this warning: the battle to beat all battles is drawing closer. The forces that have always been at work in our nation which seek to attack, undermine and dismantle the very foundations of our society ... are increasing by the day.

We need to pray, and not stop praying, that God will place the right people in positions of authority across our nation. We also need to pray for those people and their families, their Churches and their communities.

Satan will do all he can to destroy the work of God and distract, discourage and deceive the people of God. That should not evoke fear or anxiety, rather it should trigger more prayer and a sense of excitement and anticipation as God takes us all further into the front line of His kingdom ministry. He is in control and He has gone before us. Satan is not calling the shots - God is.

As Jesus declared when He walked among us, the Kingdom of God is forcefully advancing against the kingdom of this world. We are the aggressors here, and we are moving into enemy territory to take back what the devil has stolen. At every level of society, God is at work. Yes, so is Satan and the media shows us the fruit of our neglect of God every day.

But it's not all bad news. There are many committed disciples of Jesus in key positions in Government, business and community service agencies. God is doing mighty things across the world and in our own nation. He is calling us to join Him.

If we truly believe that God is in control and that His kingdom will come and His will must be done, then we also have to believe that His Spirit has been preparing us all 'for such a time as this.' This is God's battle; He will bring the victory; but He will not do it alone; He needs us to step up, seize the day and be His faithful soldiers in a thousand different ways. Each and every one of us needs to ask Him what He requires of us at such a time as this. He has a role for each and every one of us to play.

God is able - He just needs to know if we are available.

9. LEARNING TO FLY

During the bleak winter of 1940, Josephine Kuntz' husband, a house painter and textile worker, was temporarily unemployed because of the weather and a seasonal lay-off. It was a difficult time for the whole family. They literally had no money. Their daughter, Rachel, was recovering from pneumonia and wasn't doing well. The doctor insisted that 18-month-old Rachel eat a boiled egg each day, but even that was beyond their means.

"Why not pray for an egg?" suggested a young friend. They were a Church-going family, but the idea of actually praying for their needs was something they had never really considered. Josephine wasted no time. On her knees she prayed that God would provide an egg each morning for her daughter.

Later that morning Josephine heard some cackling coming from the hedge fence in front of their home. Among the bare branches sat a fat red hen. (This is a true story.) She had never seen this hen before and had no idea where it came from. She just watched in amazement as the hen laid an egg and then proceeded down the road. In a moment the hen was gone but an egg sat in her yard.

What do you do under such circumstances but thank God? The next day Josephine was startled once again to hear cackling in the hedge. The red hen came by every day for over a week and repeated this routine. Each day little Rachel had a fresh boiled egg, rich in the protein her weak body so desperately needed. The little girl got better, the weather improved, and Josephine's husband went back to work. The next morning Josephine waited by the window and watched, but the red hen did not return. She no longer needed to.

God takes care of His people, and though we don't always see it in such striking and noticeable ways, the Bible promises that He will take care of those who are His.

There is a beautifully graphic description of God's care for Israel in the book of Deuteronomy. I would like to show it to you, then pick out one aspect of it that pictures how God lovingly and caringly brings about change and maturity in the lives of His people.

> **Deuteronomy 32:9-14** *"For the LORD'S portion is His people; Jacob is the allotment of His inheritance. [Jacob here, is Israel. He is talking about the nation that came from this one man.]* *"He found him in a desert land, and in the howling waste of a wilderness; He encircled him, He cared for him, He guarded him as the pupil of His eye. [God came to the Israelites while they were in captivity in Egypt.]* *"Like an eagle that stirs up its nest, that hovers over its young, He spread His wings and caught them, He carried them on His pinions. [God stirred them up and taught them to fly in freedom as opposed to the slavery they had known for over 400 years.]* *"*
>
> *The LORD alone guided him, and there was no foreign god with him.* *"He made him ride on the high places of the earth, and he ate the produce of the field; and He made him suck honey from the rock, and oil from the flinty rock, [After God brought Israel out of Egypt, he blessed them and gave them the land of Canaan, a land* *"flowing with milk and honey."]* *Curds of cows, and milk of the flock, with fat of lambs, and rams, the breed of Bashan, and goats, with the finest of the wheat - and of the blood of grapes you drank wine."*

The passage goes on to say that, in spite of all that God did for Israel, they ultimately turned away from Him and turned to idols. We'll save that part for another day.

What I want to zero in on is verse 11, the statement that pictures God's care being like to the eagle caring for her young. *"Like an eagle that stirs up its nest, that hovers over its young, He spread His wings and caught them, He carried them on His pinions."* What a beautiful picture of how God deals with His people! A mother eagle training her young to fly. In the same way the eagle deals with her young, God dealt with Israel and deals with us today. Let's look more closely at the picture, which prompted the title of this sermon.

There are at least seven stages that a young eagle goes through when learning to fly. These stages are also evident in God's 'training' us to live the life of faith. That is the basis of the comparison. As I describe them to you, see if you recognise any of them in your life. Now I must confess that my Thesaurus really got a workout this week in order to arrive at these seven stages:

The seven stages are:

   (1) Demonstration
   (2) Discomfort
   (3) Danger
   (4) Decision
   (5) Direction Change
   (6) Doing
   (7) Deliverance

Let's look at each one now.

1. The Demonstration Stage

As the time draws near for a young eagle to begin flight training, the mother eagle will frequently push off from the perch where the nest is and hover above her young.

In response, the eaglets begin to flap their wings wildly in imitation. It's as natural and instinctive for them as breathing. That is what verse 11 is referring to when it says the eagle "*hovers*" over its young. At this stage the eaglets don't have enough feathers to fly, but they begin to develop their wing muscles. The key word here is *demonstration*. The eagle demonstrates flying for her young and they imitate her in response.

What a great picture to describe what God has done for us through Jesus! Jesus came to earth as Immanuel, "God with us," the Bible says. He demonstrated the kind of faith and life we should be leading. We read in Romans 5:8 that "*God demonstrates His own love toward us, in that while we were yet sinners, Christ died for us.*"

In 1 Timothy 1:16 we read, "*And yet for this reason I found mercy, in order that in me as the foremost, Jesus Christ might demonstrate His perfect patience, as an example for those who would believe in Him for eternal life.*" God hasn't left us to figure things out on our own. He has cared enough about us to give us a living demonstration. Remember when Jesus said, "If you've seen Me, you've seen the Father"? Jesus was and is the perfect and indispensable demonstration of how we should live the life of faith.

Throughout my lifetime, I have seen strong evangelical Churches spend lot of time in the book of Acts and the Epistles learning about the structure and purpose of the Church. That's great. We should do that and my teaching reflects that. However, I wonder at times if we have spent as much time as we should in the gospels, getting to know Jesus. Do we expend as much effort studying Matthew, Mark, Luke, and John, as we do Acts and the Epistles? It was Paul himself, the writer of most of the Epistles we have, told Timothy in 2 Timothy 2:8, "*Remember Jesus ...*"

We must not forget the One who is the embodiment and demonstration of all we are called to be! The next stage in the training of young eagles, and God training us is what I'm going to call . . . .

2. *The Discomfort Stage*

In verse 11, it says, "*Like an eagle that stirs up its nest ...*" It's one thing for those young eagles to flap their wings in the security of their down-filled home. It's quite another for them to move to the edge, look over, and imagine stepping out into thin air! Naturally, they don't want to do it.

So the adult eagle does something the young eagles won't understand until later. She begins 'stirring up' the nest! She actually begins to poke through the bottom and tear the nest apart. Very soon the young eagles will be literally forced to fly.

What often happens to us at this stage of God's teaching the faith-life is that we begin to be bothered about something. We recognize that something isn't right. We begin to get a little worried, a little anxious. There is a growing uneasiness in us. Something is out of whack and we don't quite know what it is, or if we do, we are ignoring it. Like Job, we might say, "My heart is troubled and restless..." (Job 30:27)

It can be about anything that is bothering us. A relationship. An unfulfilled dream. A stress in our lives. A fear. A weakness. An indulgence. We find ourselves thinking, "*One of these days I'm going to have to start working on that.*"

The trouble is, just as the eaglet is reluctant to get too close the edge of the nest, we, too, are reluctant to move out of our comfort zone and face whatever it is we must face. This is God stirring up our nest. He's getting us ready for change.

He wants us to face something we've not faced before, so He makes us uncomfortable. Do you know what I mean? Perhaps He wants us to face our neglected finances. Maybe it is a relationship he wants us to mend or maybe even one He wants us to break off. Whatever the case, there is a growing discomfort and uneasiness in us that is hard to ignore.

The sad thing is that some people live their entire lives in this stage. They cling to their nest like terrified eagle chicks, afraid to do anything about their problem. They'd rather live with discomfort than risk flying. "*At least the discomfort is predictable,*" they think. "*If I were to change, who knows what might happen?*"

When we find ourselves stalled at the discomfort stage, we might understand why God then brings us to the next stage of our learning.

3. The Danger Stage

Eventually, in the case of eagles, the mother eagle gets all the kids out of the nest. We know that for sure. Have you ever seen a full-grown eagle still perched in the nest of its parents, squeaking like a baby waiting for someone to bring him something to eat? No, you haven't, because one way or another, every young eagle gets booted out of the nest with nothing between them and the hard ground but air. They either learn to fly or they fall to their death. Eagles weren't meant to be nest-sitters. They were meant to fly! This danger stage isn't mentioned directly in verse 11, but it is certainly implied.

Now, what does that say to us? What I think it says is that God often allows a danger or a crisis to come into our lives that moves the issue we're ignoring off the back burner.

He sends us a wakeup call. All of a sudden, the pain gets so bad we can't ignore it anymore. Suddenly we get fired or we have an accident or a serious illness. Perhaps a spouse threatens to walk out or a creditor starts a foreclosure. Like the eagle's nest, the bottom falls out from under our lives and we realize we've got to do something – really fast!

It has probably happened to all of us. It happened to King David. In Psalm 119:67, it says, *"Before I was afflicted, I went astray, but now I keep Your word."* It took a crisis of affliction to show David the need to learn to keep God's word. If you are in a crisis right now or have had one recently, could this be the reason? Is there something you've been ignoring? Remember, God wants you to fly, not flutter in the nest. He wants you to grow up! Well, the danger stage quickly moves us on to the next stage in our training, whether we like it or not.

4. *The Decision Stage*

The nature of danger or a crisis is that it forces us off the fence or, to use our analogy, out of the nest. We have to decide, "Am I going to move ahead or am I going to retreat? Am I going to face this or try to run away? With the nest suddenly gone out from under him and the ground coming up fast, the young eagle has a choice to make. He realizes, "I have to do something - now!" So he chooses to fly or fall - he literally chooses to live or die.

God often forces us to that place, have you noticed? Especially if we are reluctant to grow or pay attention to the need to grow. If you are ignoring what you know is right, whether you are a Christian or not, what is it going to take to get you to come to a decision? Is God dealing with you right now? Is this the issue? Is it your stubbornness or neglect? When will you decide?

The next stage is so close to the decision stage that I was tempted to put them both under the same heading, but there is a difference I need to point out, so I've called the next stage . .

5. *The Direction Change Stage*

The young eagle, falling fast, has decided he must do something. What is it? He must change direction! He must start going up instead of down. When we're talking about our response to God's dealing with us, the decision stage and the direction change stage are called repentance. Repentance is a decision to turn away from evil and turn back to God. It takes place in the mind. In that way it is a decision, but since it is a decision to change, there will soon be a direction change that results.

Sometimes we are reluctant to change direction. Often it is because we haven't really made a decision to change. We may be sorry things are the way they are. We may even cry some real tears over it. But we never really change course, we don't change our minds.

Often Christians struggle with sin. They are sorry for the struggle. They don't like the prospect of the consequences. They might even come forward in Church and let the whole church know. But there is no direction change as a result.

Paul warned us in 2 Corinthians 7:10, *"For the sorrow that is according to the will of God produces a repentance without regret, leading to salvation; but the sorrow of the world produces death."*

According to that verse, you can have two people side by side who are sorry about their sins. Looking at them, they both look like they are at the same point, but they are not.

One of them has a sorrow that produces repentance - a change of direction. The other is just sorry, but there is no repentance – not change of direction.

What are we talking about? We're talking about God teaching us to fly - to live the faith life in a way that is pleasing to Him and brings us to maturity. He uses these stages to do it: Demonstration, Discomfort, Danger, Decision, Direction Change. There are still two more stages before we will be competent fliers. Bear with me, they're short.

6. The Doing Stage

The adult eagle can teach her young to fly but she cannot fly for them. They must do it themselves. Have you ever seen two adult eagles flying piggy-back? No? Neither have I – because it just doesn't happen. Flying takes effort on the part of each individual.

The Bible says in Galatians 6:5, "*Each one shall bear his own load...*" In the realm of our learning to walk the Christian walk, we must make the effort ourselves. The very common 'do nothing' religion around us is false. It is an aberration of the devil. It is a cheap substitute for the faith of the Bible. Does this mean that we get to heaven on our own merits? Not at all! But God wants us to learn to fly.

Consider this: God often gave His blessings in Scripture while the recipients of the blessings were in the midst of obedience. Remember when Israel crossed the Red Sea? Moses said, "*Move forward!*" The people obeyed. Then when the feet of the priests touched the water, it divided. When they crossed the Jordan on their way to the Promised land it was the same way. They moved forward, they put their feet in the water, in faith and obedience, and then it divided.

When Jesus cleansed the ten lepers, he told them to go present themselves to the priest. Then, "*as they were going, they were cleansed.*" (Luke 17:14). The eagle learns to fly by striving against the gravity that is pulling him down - in short, he learns to fly by flying!

This sixth step of doing is critical to the young eagle's learning to fly and it is also critical to our growing up in Christ. We need to get with it when it comes to doing the right thing. It is also critical to the final step, which I've called:

7. *The Deliverance Stage*

This one is beautiful and it's right in the text. Look again at verse 11: "*He spread His wings and caught them, He carried them on His pinions.*" I am told that the adult eagle will actually swoop down and catch her falling offspring on her back and carry them back up to the home perch. What a beautiful picture of what God does for us!

Paul told young Timothy in 2 Timothy 3:11, "*What persecutions I endured, and out of them all the Lord delivered me!*"

In Psalm 34:19 we read, "*Many are the afflictions of the righteous; but the Lord delivers him out of them all.*"

In 2 Peter 2:9, the Apostle tells us, "*The Lord knows how to rescue the godly from temptation...*"

You see, God doesn't leave us to do it on our own. It's just that we must be about the doing in order for the deliverance to come. The promise of deliverance is there. We must believe it and move ahead. We must be striving to fly even if we can't quite do it yet.

Is God teaching you how to fly? If you are a Christian, there is no doubt about it! How is your personal 'flight school' going? Are you cooperating or copping out?

Have you seen any or all of these stages of God's flight school in your life? You can be sure they are there now or will be there soon.

What is your attitude toward them? Are you focused on the goal of being able to fly and rise to the heights God created you to experience? Or are you clinging to the comfort of the nest? Be sure that God will stir it up if you are reluctant. And maybe, just maybe, you've wondered what is going on in the midst of all this. Maybe you've had some rough times recently and haven't been able to figure out why. Perhaps now you have your answer.

Be sure of these things:

- God does want you to learn to fly.
- He will put you through flight school.
- You can ignore it, but it won't stop the process.
- You can resist it, but it won't stop the process.
- You can cooperate and learn to fly for Him!

10. MOUNTAIN-MOVING FAITH

Matthew 17:14-20 *"When they came to the crowd, a man approached Jesus and knelt before him. "Lord, have mercy on my son," he said. "He has seizures and is suffering greatly. He often falls into the fire or into the water. I brought him to your disciples, but they could not heal him."*

"You unbelieving and perverse generation," Jesus replied, "how long shall I stay with you? How long shall I put up with you? Bring the boy here to me." Jesus rebuked the demon, and it came out of the boy, and he was healed at that moment. Then the disciples came to Jesus in private and asked, "Why couldn't we drive it out?"

He replied, "Because you have so little faith. Truly I tell you, if you have faith as small as a mustard seed, you can say to this mountain, 'Move from here to there,' and it will move. Nothing will be impossible for you."

Faith enough to move mountains. Mountains! What kind of mountains? Jesus is not talking about magic removals. He doesn't say that prayer can push Mount Kosciusko into the Pacific Ocean. But He is saying that faith even the size of a mustard seed can move the mountains blocking the horizons of our hopes, shadowing the light and beauty of God's love in our lives, limiting our service to Christ.

He is saying that faith the size of a mustard seed can make the improbable possible; indeed, it can make what looks impossible into a vital and radiant present reality. He is saying that faith can stand up to and move, indeed remove, the things that trap us, the stuff that scares the daylights out of us, the things that test and erode our confidence in God and make us wonder whether God is in fact able to make something of our efforts after all.

But how often it is that we lack even that tiniest amount of faith! Consider the scene here as Jesus addressed His disciples. Long before this event - back in Matthew 10:8 - Jesus had given the disciples full authority to "*cure the sick, raise the dead, cleanse the lepers, cast out demons.*"

By this time they should be performing healings, cleansings, miracles, with absolute confidence and faith! Yet, on this day, they are unable to heal even this little boy. So it is Jesus who must step in and do the miracle once again. And it is Jesus once again confronting his well-meaning followers that they are still a "faithless" generation.

These words remind us of other events; in particular, we recall the events recorded in Luke 8, where Jesus and the disciples, on a boat on the Sea of Galilee, are caught suddenly by a violent windstorm; and the disciples rush in to wake Jesus, crying, "*Master, we are perishing!*"

There, too, Jesus responds by asking his followers, simply: "*Where is your faith?*" And now, once again, Jesus confronts the disciples with the same question: "*Where is your faith?*" He could not be any clearer: In verse 20, He tells them, "*The reason you could not cure this young boy is* because of your little faith." Then, Jesus gives the rest of the story: "*For truly I tell you, if you have faith the size of a mustard seed, you will say to this mountain, 'Move from here to there,' and it will move; and nothing will be impossible for you.*"

The faith to move a mountain! How are we to understand that? Did Jesus mean that, literally, his disciples, with a little faith, ought to be able to stare up at the Mount of Transfiguration, from which they had just come down a little earlier that day, and command it to pick up and move to the other side of the Sea of Galilee, and it would be done?

No, I don't think that was exactly Jesus' intention; nowhere in the Gospels do we see Jesus rearranging geography just for the sake of performing a miracle. There was another, very real mountain looming in front of the disciples that day; specifically, it was the mountain of healing that sick boy that had been brought to them. And Jesus declared to them, "*If you had even the tiniest bit of faith, this mountain will be one that you can conquer.*"

The reason that the disciples should have been able to heal this boy, with a little faith, is because Jesus had commanded them, and Jesus had given them the authority, to do just that. With faith even the size of a mustard seed, they should have been able to do everything that Jesus had given them to do.

In that respect, we can place ourselves in the disciples' shoes. For God has given each and every one of us a job to do, a mission to perform, and Jesus has given us full authority to act in his name as we carry out our calling. That is the 'mountain' that lies before you, and me, today! And with faith even as big as this tiny mustard seed, that mountain will move before our very eyes, even today!

In some respects, every person's 'mountain' is a little bit different. That's because every one of us is an individual, unique in certain respects, given unique abilities and talents by God. So, each of us is called by God to do something different. But the thing we must do today is realize that whatever it is that God has called us to do, God has also given us full authority to do just that - just like Jesus gave His disciples full authority to heal the sick and cast out demons. And we must, today, reach back and find the faith - not necessarily superhuman faith; just the smallest bit will do - faith that we are fully, completely able to do exactly what God has given us to do.

Faith that, when the time comes, when we need it to happen most, that "*mountain*" will give way before us. What is your mountain? It may be a mountain of sharing Christ with a person very close to you. It may be a mountain of taking a stand for Christ in a new, more powerful way. It may be a mountain of accepting new responsibilities, a role of leadership, in your service to Christ.

It may be a mountain of giving that last little area of your life, the one little compartment that you've not been willing to part with yet, giving even that part of your life completely over to Christ.

It may be a mountain of refusing to sit quietly any longer while your colleagues, acquaintances, co-workers, trample the name of Christ.

Your task today is to find just enough faith to know that you're not just fighting alone, as a 'loose cannon' on the deck, but rather that God has empowered you with full authority to tackle this mountain, and that this mountain can begin to give way before you even today!

There are other mountains that lie in common before all of us. That's because there are some things that Christ has exhorted all of us, as his followers in 21st century Australia, to do. For one thing, he has exhorted us to "*be not conformed to this world but be transformed by the renewing of [our] minds.*" (Romans 12:2). He has exhorted us to "*go and make disciples.*" (Matthew 28:20).

And the faith-inspiring part of this is, He has given us full authority to do these things; He's given us the authority to serve and conquer in Jesus' name. If only we can muster up that tiniest bit of faith, these mountains will not continue to block our path; they will move aside for us.

There's even another category of 'mountains' that may be standing before you today. These are the mountains which shout back at you - taunt you, even saying, "*You don't stand a chance in getting past* me!" Mountains of self-rejection; mountains of low self-esteem; mountains of doubt; mountains of discouragement brought into sharp focus by past failures.

Once again, the promise holds: Christ has given you full authority to get past these mountains; and with faith even as small as a mustard seed, you can do just that. You can do it because Christ promises you that you are accepted - by Him.

You can do it because Christ promises that He can make all things new - even a life that's been marked by failures, disappointments, rebellion, anything at all. God can begin to remove these mountains from before you even today!

"*Faith the size of a mustard seed.*" It's so significant that this is all that it takes - for is there anyone among us today that honestly perceives himself or herself as having "*great, big faith*"? No, we always manage to see ourselves as the weakling. We always manage to pick out someone else that seems to have "*so much more faith than I do.*"

The promise of God here is that's not important! God will work even with weaklings! Faith, according to the writer of the book of Hebrews, is "*the assurance of things hoped for, the conviction of things not seen.*"

And Abraham is lifted up as an example of faith! But do you really think Abraham viewed himself as a possessor of great faith? No. I imagine that Abraham stumbled through a lot of his life, saying to himself, "*I can't believe I'm doing this!*"

As he followed God's guidance into a strange new land; as he trusted God's promise for a child; as he followed God up the mountainside, presumably to sacrifice his only son Isaac - I'm sure that the last thing on Abraham's mind was this "great faith" that he supposedly possessed.

And for you too, as you stumble headlong into life's challenges, a 'superhero of faith' might be the last thing you would consider calling yourself. The promise of Christ, though, is that we don't have to be superheros! We simply need to muster up faith the size of a tiny little seed - and the mountains will begin to move.

"Faith the size of a mustard seed." What little step might you and I need to take in order for that kind of faith to take root today? It may mean that you simply need to stop complaining, *"This will never work."* It may mean that you simply stop making excuses today. It may mean that you simply need to stop hesitating today to make that one little commitment that's been gnawing at your conscience. It doesn't take much to produce faith the size of a mustard seed - but until we do just that little bit, the mountains will continue to stand firmly in place in front of us.

Do you believe that Christ has given us, His people, a job to do? Do you believe that Christ has empowered you to do that job? Do you believe that Christ has empowered you to serve Him? Do you believe that, if Christ has given you a job to do in service to Him, He is able to move any mountains that might stand between you and the completion of that service?

But maybe you still doubt. Maybe your mountain just seems too large, too immovable. Perhaps you've been praying for years for a breakthrough in your family, in your finances, in your health, and nothing has changed.

You might say, *"I've tried faith. I've prayed, I've trusted - and the mountain is still there."* Let me encourage you: Jesus didn't say that the mountain would move instantly; He said that nothing will be impossible for you. Sometimes, faith is not just the immediate miracle - it's the persistent belief that God is still working, even when you can't see it.

Do you remember the story of the persistent widow in Luke's gospel? Jesus told this parable, *"... to show them that they should always pray and not give up."* (Luke 18:1). The widow kept coming to the judge day after day, and though he was unjust, he finally granted her justice.

Jesus concluded, *"Will not God bring about justice for his chosen ones, who cry out to him day and night? ...However, when the Son of Man comes, will he find faith on the earth?"* (Luke 18:7-8). In other words, real mountain-moving faith is not only about believing once - it's about not giving up. It's about praying and persisting, even when the mountain doesn't move at first glance.

You see, sometimes the mountain isn't removed in front of us - it's climbed. And God gives us strength for the climb. The Apostle Paul, a man of extraordinary faith, dealt with a *"thorn in the flesh"* that wasn't removed, even after he pleaded with the Lord three times.

Yet God responded, *"My grace is sufficient for you, for my power is made perfect in weakness."* (2 Corinthians 12:9). Mountain-moving faith sometimes trusts that even if the mountain remains, God's grace is enough to carry us over it.

While we're talking about mustard seed faith, let's not forget what Jesus says in another passage about that same seed.

In Matthew 13:31-32, He says: *"The kingdom of heaven is like a mustard seed, which a man took and planted in his field. Though it is the smallest of all seeds, yet when it grows, it is the largest of garden plants and becomes a tree..."* Not only does mustard seed faith move mountains, it grows into something that gives shelter and strength to others. Your small act of faith today may not only change your life - but it may also be the very thing that gives others courage to believe tomorrow.

Are you willing to follow Christ right now, and begin working at that service to him, believing that, when the time comes, he will be faithful to roll that mountain out of the way? If you can answer "yes" to these questions, then you are indeed ready to generate faith the size of a mustard seed; faith that, like that tiny seed, can grow and grow, until it becomes something life-changing, even superhuman!

"The Little Engine That Could" approached the base of that ominous mountain full of doubt and fear. Could he make it up and over? You know the story – he headed into the side of that mountain, crying with determination, *"I think I can, I think I can,"* and slowly, the little engine began to scale the mountain. Inch by inch, his confidence grew, until finally he was able to triumphantly cry out, *"I know I can, I know I can!"*

As you approach whatever mountain may be standing before you today, you may be tempted to say, "No way." It may seem like a lifetime away, the prospect of being able to cry out, *"I know I can!"*

Well, can you at least say with faithful determination, *"I think I can"* - and plunge in, with that much faith? That's all that's required of us today; that tiny amount of faith that allows us at least to say, *"I think it's possible" - and I'm willing to follow God and find out! "*

That may not sound like much of a commitment; it may sound weak- but is it not a giant leap from where we may be right now, saying, "*No way is that possible.*" Simply commit today to be willing to see the possibilities; commit to step forward with Christ, whichever direction his next step may fall - and before long you'll be amazed at how those mountains begin to fall; and before you know it, you'll be shouting out, along with the Little Engine That Could: "*I know I can!*"

Also, don't underestimate the testimony that results when your mountain moves - or when you have the grace to climb it. When God does what only God can do, the world takes notice. That's why Jesus said in Matthew 5:16, *"Let your light shine before others, that they may see your good deeds and glorify your Father in heaven."* Your faith in action, your small steps forward, your refusal to give up when things are hard - these all speak louder than sermons.

This is especially important in today's culture. We live in an age of scepticism, where people are not always moved by arguments, but they are moved by authenticity. They are moved by people who live with courage, hope, and peace - even when life is difficult. They are moved by people whose lives are marked by something different, something resilient - something divine. That something is faith. And when we walk by faith, not by sight, we become living witnesses to the reality and power of God.

So let's get practical. What might "mustard seed faith" look like for you this week? It could mean sending that message of forgiveness. It might mean volunteering for a ministry you've always felt too inadequate to join. It could mean opening your Bible again after a long dry spell. It might mean speaking up about your faith in a conversation where silence would be easier.

These are not grand, headline-making moves, but they are 'mustard seed' moments, and when you trust God enough to act, those seeds begin to grow.

Mountain-moving faith simply says, "*Nothing – nothing at all can cut us off from God; nothing can separate us from the love of God that is in Jesus Christ.*" Faith, the size of a mustard seed, faith in the steadfast, enduring, tenacious love of God; faith in Christ's ability to bring to completion whatever good work it may be that He's started in you, in me: Jesus isn't kidding, it is faith enough to move mountains.

So let me leave you with a challenge - and a promise. The challenge is this: identify one mountain that stands before you right now. Name it. Bring it before God. And ask Him for the faith - even mustard seed faith - to face it, to pray about it, to act upon it. And the promise is this: that nothing will be impossible with God. Jesus doesn't speak in maybes or ifs here. He says with clarity and confidence, *"It will move. Nothing will be impossible for you."*

The mountain-moving faith that Jesus talks about is not the absence of fear - it's the presence of trust. It is not the denial of difficulty - it is the embrace of divine authority. And it's available to every single one of us. Not tomorrow. Not when you feel you are 'ready.' But right now.

Will you believe that God can move your mountain? Will you believe that He can use your life to make a difference in the world around you? Will you believe that with Him, nothing is impossible?

Then stand tall, even if your knees are shaking, seize the day and speak to that mountain! Watch what God will do.

11. TRUE WORSHIP

What is true worship? If you think about that question for long, you will find that there must be many answers to it because there are so many churches doing so many different things and calling it worship. If you were to sit in on a different service every Sunday morning, you would find that some churches are very different in style from other churches.

You may find what is called the 'high church' style. There you will experience considerable formality and ritual. Sometimes choirs will march into the sanctuary in a great processional. The Ministers may wear long robes. The atmosphere is generally sombre. Things are always done exactly the same way without any deviation.

Then there is what some call the 'low church' style. Here there is often no printed order of worship, although they have their unwritten order. The atmosphere is very informal. Unexpected things happen and are not considered interruptions. The service is not sombre, but lively and can sometimes seem too lively.

Then, of course, there are a variety of styles in between those two. Which is right? Obviously, the one you personally prefer is the right one - at least in your eyes. The truth is that they could all be right or all be wrong, and whether they are or not, has little to do with the style but everything to do with the worshipper.

Many people feel that God is moving in His church in a fresh way today. They feel that a part of this fresh move of God is a restoration of true praise and worship. I think this is true. If it is true, then we ought to understand what God is emphasising. After all, praise and worship are His ideas.

A careful reading of the Scriptures will reveal that God has created us to worship and exhorts us to worship Him. Just in Psalm 150, one of our shortest Psalms, we are exhorted 12 times to praise the Lord.

> *Praise the Lord! Praise God in His sanctuary;*
> *Praise Him in His mighty expanse.*
> *Praise Him for His mighty deeds;*
> *Praise Him according to His excellent greatness.*
> *Praise Him with trumpet sound;*
> *Praise Him with harp and lyre.*
> *Praise Him with timbrel and dancing;*
> *Praise Him with stringed instruments and pipe.*
> *Praise Him with loud cymbals;*
> *Praise Him with resounding cymbals.*
> *Let everything that has breath praise the Lord.*
> *Praise the Lord!*

God exhorts us to praise Him, and God is saying to His church today, as He has said so often in the past, that we are called to praise our Lord. When I began to understand the emphasis God places on praise, I also began to wonder why. Why does God place so much emphasis on praise directed toward Himself? It seemed strange. Personally, I may want people to praise me because I need my ego to be stroked. But God has no inferiority complex. He does not have an ego which needs to be massaged.

He doesn't need praise so that He can feel better about Himself. Why then would God want us to praise Him? I believe the answer lies not in God, but in us. God doesn't want us to praise Him because He needs our praise. God wants us to praise Him because we need what praise can do in our lives. God doesn't need to be praised, but we need to praise Him, because praise and worship does something in us and for us!

God exhorts us to worship because praise and worship is an imperative for every Christian. This means that it is absolutely essential for us to engage in praise and worship. It is essential because God created us to praise Him.

We must also remember that praise is not only about words or songs - it is a declaration of allegiance. In praising God, we are reminding ourselves and those around us of who truly reigns. In a world full of distractions and idols vying for our attention, intentional worship places God back at the centre. It's an act of realignment.

Every time we offer heartfelt praise, we are proclaiming: *"God is King. He is worthy. He is good."* In this way, praise becomes a spiritual discipline that keeps our hearts anchored in truth. Worship renews our minds and shields us from the lies and values of the world around us. This is why Satan despises true worship - because it dethrones self, silences fear and exalts Christ alone.

We were created to praise and worship God. Wherever you find human beings, you find them worshiping something or someone. Whether in the darkest jungle or right here in civilised western society, people are worshiping. They may not be worshiping in some formal sense in a house of worship, but they are worshiping, nonetheless. In the jungle they may be worshiping a rock or a tree or their dead ancestors.

In Australia they may be worshiping at some other altar. It seems that there is a need for human beings to reach out beyond themselves and give honour and adoration to something larger. Human beings will have a god, even if it is not the true God. Of course, God desires for us to become true worshipers who are worshiping the one true God.

> **John 4:23-24** *"Yet a time is coming and has now come when the true worshipers will worship the Father in spirit and truth, for they are the kind of worshipers the Father seeks. God is spirit, and his worshipers must worship in spirit and in truth."*

God has called us to be these true worshipers. He exhorts us to worship Him in spirit and truth. Indeed, the text indicates that God seeks those kind of worshipers.

To worship God in spirit and truth means that we worship the true God. It means that our worship should come from a place of honesty and integrity. It means that our worship should be spiritual, full of passion, engaging the whole person, and supernatural in nature.

This is the highest calling for every believer. In fact, Christians are compared with Old Testament priests. In the Old Testament, priests offered sacrifices to God. According to the New Testament, we are all priests who offer sacrifices as well.

In the Old Testament the priests would offer animals as a burnt offering. As New Testament priests, we offer a different kind of sacrifice, but it is a sacrifice, nonetheless.

> **1 Peter 2:4-5, 9** *"As you come to him, the living Stone - rejected by men but chosen by God and precious to him - you also, like living stones, are being built into a spiritual house to be a holy priesthood, offering spiritual sacrifices acceptable to God through Jesus Christ."*
>
> *"... but you are a chosen people, a royal priesthood, a holy nation, a people belonging to God, that you may declare the praises of him who called you out of darkness into his wonderful light."*

Here we are told that we are a royal priesthood, and that our job is to offer up spiritual sacrifices. What are these spiritual sacrifices? This priestly role means that worship is not just the responsibility of the song leader or the pastor - it belongs to every believer. Whether you are in the pew or at home, your voice matters.

The priesthood of all believers means that each of us can come boldly before God's throne (Hebrews 4:16) and offer our worship. This is especially important in a culture that often reduces worship to performance or platform.

True worship isn't about a stage - it's about surrender and God is not looking for polished presentations; He's looking for hearts that adore Him.

That's why Paul urges us in Romans 12:1 to offer our bodies as *"living sacrifices, holy and pleasing to God - this is your true and proper worship."* True worship is sacrificial - it involves giving God the best of who we are.

> **Hebrews 13:15** *"Through Him then, let us continually offer up a sacrifice of praise to God, that is, the fruit of lips that give thanks to His name."*

The spiritual sacrifices that we are to offer are sacrifices of praise. What is this praise? It is the fruit of our lips. In other words, it is verbal, vocal praise. The passage in Hebrews corresponds to another passage in Hosea.

> **Hosea 14:1-2** *"Return, O Israel, to the LORD your God. Your sins have been your downfall! Take words with you and return to the LORD. Say to him: "Forgive all our sins and receive us graciously, that we may offer the fruit of our lips."*

This is a high calling. Entering into true praise and worship should not be optional for any of us. It is a part of our very fabric as human beings made in the image of God. It is imperative that we come to understand and practice true biblical praise and worship.

But what are the consequences of practicing true praise and worship? We have already mentioned that we engage in praise and worship, not for God's benefit as much as for our benefit. So we might ask what praise and worship does for us. Why do we need to praise and worship God? Let's look briefly at five reasons we need to do so.

1. God made us to worship: Worship is built into the very design of our being. Just as lungs are made to breathe and hearts are made to beat, our souls are made to worship. When we don't worship God, we don't cease being worshipers - we simply redirect that worship elsewhere. That "elsewhere" might be wealth, success, relationships, or even ourselves. Paul describes this spiritual misdirection: *"They exchanged the truth about God for a lie and worshiped and served created things rather than the Creator."* (Romans 1:25)

We are always worshiping something, which is why God's call to worship Him is both gracious and protective. He knows that our souls will wither when they worship what is unworthy. But when we worship the One Who made us and redeemed us, our spirits flourish. Worship is not just a Sunday activity - it is the very rhythm of the redeemed life.

2. God is worthy of our worship: In Revelation 4:11 we read, *"You are worthy, our Lord and God, to receive glory and honour and power, for you created all things, and by your will they were created and have their being."* God is worthy of our praise because He is our Creator and our Lord.

Throughout the book of Revelation we catch a glimpse of heavenly worship. John's vision transports us into heaven itself and there we see that a chief activity is praise.

> **Revelation 5:11-12** *"Then I looked and heard the voice of many angels, numbering thousands upon thousands, and ten thousand times ten thousand. They encircled the throne and the living creatures and the elders. In a loud voice they sang: "Worthy is the Lamb, who was slain, to receive power and wealth and wisdom and strength and honour and glory and praise!"*

> **Revelation 7:11-12** *"All the angels were standing around the throne and around the elders and the four living creatures. They fell down on their faces before the throne and worshiped God, saying: "Amen! Praise and glory and wisdom and thanks and honour and power and strength be to our God for ever and ever. Amen!"*

We had better get used to praise and worship on this earth because we will be doing a lot of it in heaven! But we should do it here because our God is worthy of our worship.

3. Worship brings us into God's presence: Praise and worship is the path leading to God. We are told in Psalm 100:4 to, *"Enter His gates with thanksgiving and His courts with praise."* As we praise and worship God, we shift our focus from ourselves and our situation to Him. This makes us aware of His presence.

This brings us into communion with Him. We become aware of His glory and greatness, of His majesty and power. We turn our attention from lesser things and focus on that which is the ultimate, our Lord and God. Praise and worship transport us into the very presence of the living God. It places us in a position where we can hear from Him and receive His ministry.

The Bible gives us many different examples of how worship can usher people into divine encounters. In 2 Chronicles 20, when King Jehoshaphat faced a vast army, he appointed singers to go before the army, praising the Lord. As they worshiped, God set ambushes against their enemies, and the battle was won without a single sword being lifted. Worship shifted the atmosphere from fear to faith, from defeat to deliverance.

When we enter God's presence through praise, we also enter His power. Anxiety, despair, and confusion often melt in the presence of the Almighty. That's why Isaiah 61:3 speaks of God giving His people "a garment of praise instead of a spirit of heaviness (despair)." Praise is not just a celebration after the breakthrough – it is often the catalyst for the breakthrough.

4. Worship gives us God's perspective on our situation: Because we are transported, as it were, into His presence, we now behold His greatness and become aware of His ability to deal with our situation.

When we had our eyes on our situation or problem, it all looked pretty large. When we shift our attention, however, from ourselves to the God Who created this universe, then our whole life and the circumstances which surround us are seen in their proper perspective.

Some issue or problem may have appeared huge to us while we were focusing only on it, but when we began to behold the glory, majesty, might and power of God, suddenly the problem didn't look as big anymore. Looking at the problem in light of the majesty and ability of God makes the problem look solvable. Praise and worship give us God's perspective on our situation, which is what we all need.

5. Worship changes us: Praise and worship changes our attitudes and thinking. It is impossible to become one who truly praises and worships God and still be sour and cynical. Praise and worship will transform our character. It will make us people of hope, people of faith.

Through praise and worship, God will do a mighty work in us. That alone is enough reason to become one who places great emphasis on praise and worship.

If you are sad and sorry and cynical and negative and see all the things that are wrong with your life and your world ... then you need to get your eyes off the rubbish dump and onto the sunrise.

You need to find yourself lost in praise and adoration and worship of a God Who has promised to never leave you or forsake you. You will be amazed at how quickly your perspective on life changes.

One of the profound transformations worship brings is a softening of the heart. When we consistently draw near to God in worship, He begins to shape our affections, desires, and character. We begin to love what He loves and hate what He hates. Psalm 115 warns that those who make idols *"will be like them."*

In contrast, when we worship the living God, we become more like Him. We reflect His mercy, humility, and truth. Worship reorients our identity - it reminds us we are children of the King, not slaves to the world.

That's why spending time in God's presence isn't a duty, but a source of spiritual vitality. It's not just about singing songs - it's about being reshaped by glory.

You and I have been called to lift up our voices in praise and worship. We are New Testament priests, commanded to offer up the sacrifice of praise to God continually. Sometimes it is more of a sacrifice than at other times.

But at all times we ought to be people of praise, because our God is worthy of our praise, and because we receive so much through praise. If true worship becomes our first priority, we will be amazed at how easy it is to truly seize the day!

12. THE TIME IS NOW!

2 Corinthians 6:2 *"Now is the acceptable time."*

It should be said that although God is the Master of time, we are not. In fact, we are pretty much the slaves of time. The clock is always ticking, and there is never quite enough time left. It seems that we are always running out of time. Time passes so quickly. Deadlines are upon us before we know it and we feel the intense pressure and stress that these fixed moments in time cause us. If only we could in some way s-t-r-e-t-c-h time. But we cannot.

Many years ago now, the founder of Microsoft, Bill Gates, who has amassed billions of dollars in personal wealth, was asked what was one thing that he really wanted. He replied without hesitation and said, *"More time."* We would all like more time. Time is a ruthless taskmaster.

But for all of our frustrations concerning time, we must remember that time may be less real than we think. Do you suppose that God has a calendar in heaven? What kind of watch do you think God wears on His wrist? There is no time as we know it in heaven. There God lives in eternity, which is not time drawn out but timelessness. The concept of time is a convention for the benefit of mankind so that our lives can experience some sense of successiveness, order predictability.

And yet, what is most remarkable is that Jesus - God incarnate - stepped into our time. The eternal, infinite One entered our temporal, finite history. He who existed outside of time chose to be born in a manger, at a specific moment in time, live in a particular generation, and die at a precise hour. The Gospel of John captures this with repeated references to *"His hour."*

Jesus often said, *"My time has not yet come,"* and then, as the Cross drew near, He said, *"The hour has come."* (John 17:1). His life was not ruled by time, but it was attuned to God's timing. What a mystery - that the timeless Son of God would submit Himself to the ticking of earthly hours in order to save us!

That alone tells us something profound: if Jesus lived within time for our sake, then how we use our time must matter deeply to God.

Time certainly has a definite impact in all of our lives, and we deal differently with time in different stages of our lives. When we were young, we tended to wish time away. We were always waiting for something - for some future event to happen. It might have been a birthday, or a vacation, or Christmas.

The week before Christmas is always the longest week of the year for young children as they wait to see what is inside those pretty parcels. Time seems to move incredibly slow when we are young. And when we were young the time between the present and that longed-for event was always wished away. We were always wanting to grow up more quickly.

To some degree we still do this. But this is a false dealing with time. By wishing for some future day to arrive we may miss the present reality entirely. But we still wish. We wish for the day that we will graduate from high school, then college. We wish for the day we will be married to the one we love. We wish for the day we will begin that new job. We wish for the day we can buy that new home. We wish for the day when our children will be on their own. We wish for the day when we will retire.

These are all good milestones, but what about today? We can spend most of our lives thinking about the days over which we have no real control, whilst ignoring the one day we can control in a limited way: that's today. We are exhorted to seize the day - and that day can only ever be today!

When we are always living for some future event, we are wasting today. If we never learn to live in the present we will look back on our lives and conclude that our days were wasted waiting for the next thing to happen. While time may not be real in the ultimate sense, it is certainly not an illusion. It is something with which we must deal and deal effectively. The Bible deals with it. God calls each of us to deal with it.

So in this closing chapter, I want us to reflect for a moment on the three most common designations of time with which you and I deal every day: yesterday, today and tomorrow.

Yesterday

In thinking about time, we must think clearly about the past. It should go without saying that the past is past. What we have done is done and there is nothing we can do about it. And people who can allow the past to be past are blessed indeed. As I dealt with in detail back in chapter 2, the past can bind us, it can imprison us. Some people live in the past and are therefore imprisoned by it. T

hat is not to say that there is anything wrong with memories. In fact, good memories are exceedingly valuable. But the memories of our failures and our fears, and the times we were hurt by others; these are the things that can drag us down. In one sense, this sense, we really do need to let the past go.

You may recall a story I have shared before about a ministry colleague of mine, Dr Ken Blue. Ken's grandfather's farm in the USA was a place where Ken used to spend holidays when he was a child. In the paddock next to the house there was this huge pear tree which Ken used to climb and sit at the top for hours. He felt like he could see forever from up there. It was his special place.

Many years later, after Ken was married with his own children and living a long way from the farm, his grandfather called him one day with some bad news. A huge storm had hit the farm and the magnificent old pear tree had been uprooted. He knew how special that tree was to Ken and so he asked him if he wanted to see it one last time before it was removed. Ken drove out to the farm, reflecting on the way about the special times he had in that tree.

As soon as he arrived, Ken and his grandfather walked over to the next paddock and they both just stood there in silence next to this majestic old tree, which was totally uprooted and lying on the ground. Ken finally said, through tears, *"So what do we do now grandfather?"* The wise old man put his arm on Ken's shoulder and said, "Son, we pick the fruit and burn the rest." That one statement remained with Ken the rest of his life and became a powerful principle for living.

There's a well-known story of Clara Barton, founder of the American Red Cross, who was once reminded of a cruel thing someone had done to her years earlier.

She seemed not to recall it. *"Don't you remember what they did to you?"* her friend asked. "No," Barton replied firmly, *"I distinctly remember forgetting it."* That is the kind of spiritual wisdom we need when it comes to the past.

We don't pretend it didn't happen - but we choose not to let it define us or control us. We choose to 'remember forgetting it' in order to live fully today.

As we face each new chapter in our lives and reflect on the journey which brought us to that point, we need to be able to 'pick the fruit' - that is, learn from the past; grow from our mistakes; cherish the memories; be thankful for the good times; but then we need to 'burn the rest' - all of those disappointments, failures and things we wish had happened differently.

We have to move forward into the 'new day' God has prepared for us and not stand there beside a dead tree longing for a day which has passed. In another sense, however, the past is not dead at all. And it should not be.

The past is very much alive in us. The past has shaped us. It has made us, to a certain degree, who we are. Because of our experiences in the past, our character has been formed the way it is. So in a real sense the past is present with us every moment.

How do you view your past? Is it something that still haunts you, or is it something that helps you? Are there unresolved issues in your past that you need to deal with this week as you say farewell to what is behind you?

Are there people in your past you need to contact in order to make something right? Are there past sins you need to confess and lay to rest as you claim God's forgiveness?

The past is past, but it is not dead. We must deal with the past effectively if we are to live in the present happily.

Tomorrow

In thinking about time another thing we try to deal with is the future. Our yesterdays are behind us. Our tomorrows are not yet here. Indeed, tomorrow never comes. When it gets here, it is today. It should be said about the future, that it is uncertain.

There is no guarantee that we will ever see any point in what we call the future. Our lives could end at any time. There is no guarantee that we will live to be ninety, or eighty, or seventy, or fifty, or even thirty.

John Keats, Percy Shelley and Lord Byron were all very prominent, and famous 18th century romantic poets, but I wonder if you know that Keats died at twenty-five, Shelley at thirty and Byron at thirty-six.

History is filled with people who met unexpected tragedy. Most of us know of someone who died unexpectedly at a very early age. None of us have a guarantee of tomorrow. Tomorrow is not even ours anyway. God holds our future in His hands.

This does not mean that we do not think about the future or plan for the future. We should certainly do both of those things. We should consider the possibilities for the future and we should also be prepared for what the future may hold. But we should think realistically about the future if we are to live effectively in the present.

The future can give us hope. Today and every day, we face the beginning of a whole new chapter in our journey. What will that new chapter hold for us? We certainly hope that it holds good things. One thing it does hold is the promise that it may be better than the past.

It also holds the promise that things needing change in our lives may in fact be changed. While there are no guarantees, it does hold the promise and the hope for good things.

On the other hand, the future can also give us a false hope. It can provide a false sense of security and thereby keep us from living effectively in the present. By assuming that we do have the guarantee of tomorrow we can post-pone many of the things we need to be doing today. This false hope that we will be able to accomplish something 'tomorrow' provides many people with the excuse they want so they can put off the very thing they need to do today.

I have met so many people who attempt to live in the future. They are going to do great things when they get around to it. When they have time, they are going to become more involved in things that really matter. When this happens, or that happens, then they will begin. They will do it later, tomorrow, next week, next month, someday. The fact is that the time never comes, the situation is never right, tomorrow never arrives.

I heard a story once of an Elder visiting newcomers to the community. The wife began to attend Church but this man always put the Elder off. He said that he would come to church just as soon as he got straightened out.

Each time the Elder would see him, the man would make the same reply. As soon as he got straightened out, he would come to Church. Finally, the man died. The Elder was called upon to speak at the funeral. As he stood behind the pulpit in the Church sanctuary looking down at the coffin with the man inside, he thought quietly to himself, *"Well, he finally kept his promise ... to come to Church when he got straightened out."* Be careful not to let your promises be fulfilled the same way.

Procrastination is one of the most debilitating, life-draining condition any human being can suffer from.

Today

The bottom line of the whole matter is that we only have today. Today is all we have. This is why the Scripture says that now is the acceptable time. It is an affirmation that we live in the present. The past is gone. The future may never arrive. But the present is here. Now is the only time we can accept and it is the only time acceptable to God. The question we must answer is this: What are we going to do with now?

How are you spending now? Are you either living in the past or the future? Are there things you have been putting off until tomorrow - things which you should be doing today? Are you sitting back thinking that there will come that perfect situation which will enable you to be involved? It will never come.

This is the message we need to hear as we enter every new chapter in our lives. Don't wait until the calendar reaches a particular date ... and after it does ... don't look to the next milestone before you take charge of the present and seize the day, because today is the only day we have. Thank God for the past. Thank God for whatever future there is awaiting us. But live now.

We must live now in terms of our personal lives and also in terms of the Church. You see, we cannot simply wait for the future to come upon us. If the next chapter of our lives is going to be lived for Jesus, it must be lived one day at a time. Every day will be today. The only time we will have to live will be now.

So, what are the issues with which you need to deal today? Are there sins you need to confess today? *"Today is the day of salvation."* God forgave those sins over 2,000 years ago in the broken body of Jesus and the experience of that forgiveness awaits you today if you will come to Him.

In terms of your commitment to your local Church, what is the Lord calling you to do today? Are you involved, committed, active, dependable, pressing-in, dedicated, and alive? Are you involved in the ministry of your Church by giving of your time, talents, and resources? Without your support, your local Church might just as well close its doors – like many are every week across the world.

The late missionary Jim Elliott once wrote in his journal, *"Wherever you are, be all there. Live to the hilt every situation you believe to be the will of God."* Elliott was a man who gave his life for the Gospel, but he didn't do it in grand future dreams - he lived every single day with intentionality. He poured his time and energy into the present, because he knew that today might be all he had.

What is the Lord touching in your life today? What will you do about it? Whatever you do, you must do it now. Because, my friends, now is the only time you have and the only time you will ever have.

This is how we 'seize the day' and that seems to be a fitting place to end this book. I would really encourage you to review these 12 chapters in the coming days and allow the Spirit of God to give you the tools you need in every area of life so you might be able to embrace everything which God has prepared for you – every day!

www.ingramcontent.com/pod-product-compliance
Lightning Source LLC
Chambersburg PA
CBHW071248070526
44583CB00017B/2378